Five-Star
COMFORT FOOD

Five-Star COMFORT FOOD

INSPIRATIONAL RECIPES FOR THE HOME COOK

RICH KOMEN

WITH

JAMES BEARD AWARD-WINNING AUTHOR

JAMES O. FRAIOLI

FOOD PHOTOGRAPHY BY

TUCKER + HOSSLER

Skyhorse Publishing

Culinary Book Creations

Published in 2024 by Skyhorse Publishing in association with Culinary Book Creations LLC. All rights reserved. No part of this book may be reproduced in any manner without the express written consent of the publisher, except in the case of brief excerpts in critical reviews or articles. All inquiries should be addressed to Skyhorse Publishing, 307 West 36th Street, 11th Floor, New York, NY 10018 and/or james@culinarybookcreations.com at Culinary Book Creations.

Skyhorse Publishing books may be purchased in bulk at special discounts for sales promotion, corporate gifts, fund-raising, or educational purposes. Special editions can also be created to specifications. For details, contact the Special Sales Department, Skyhorse Publishing, 307 West 36th Street, 11th Floor, New York, NY 10018 or info@skyhorsepublishing.com.

Skyhorse® and Skyhorse Publishing® are registered trademarks of Skyhorse Publishing, Inc.®, a Delaware corporation. Culinary Book Creations® is a registered trademark of Culinary Book Creations, a Washington LLC corporation.

Visit our websites at www.skyhorsepublishing.com and www.culinarybookcreations.com.

10 9 8 7 6 5 4 3 2 1

Library of Congress Cataloging-in-Publication Data is available on file.

Cover design by The Book Designers & Kai Texel
Cover photo credit: Tucker + Hossler Photography
Production: James O. Fraioli, Culinary Book Creations, LLC
Designers: Alan Dino Hebel and Ian Koviak, The Book Designers
Editor for Culinary Book Creations: Varsana Tikovsky
Editor for Skyhorse Publishing: Nicole Frail

Print ISBN: 978-1-5107-8011-8
Ebook ISBN: 978-1-5107-8030-9

Printed in China

CONTENTS

INTRODUCTION BY RICH KOMEN 1

PASS THE APPETIZERS, PLEASE 9

SALADS, SOUPS & A CHOWDER 29

PASTA & NOODLE BOWLS 51

BEEF, BEEF & MORE BEEF 77

CHICKEN MANY WAYS 115

PORK FROM EVERYWHERE 161

FRESH OFF THE DOCK .181

EGGS & RICE, POTATOES & VEGGIES 201

PUDDING & FOUR SWEET PIES 235

Acknowledgments 248
Metric Conversions 249
Index 250

INTRODUCTION

Hello. I'm the founder of Restaurants Unlimited, Inc., a fast-growing restaurant company from the 1980s. During the first two formative decades of our existence, my company had more than thirty restaurants and over a hundred Cinnabon bakeries. But let me step back.

The year was 1960. I had earlier graduated with an accounting degree from the University of Washington. While working for a wholesale grocery supplier in Seattle, I learned my alma mater was looking for a new concession vendor at Husky Stadium for their football games. I was excited to give it a shot. With a thousand dollars in savings, I met with members of the school's athletic department to learn more about taking over the concession business. I was twenty-eight years old and didn't have any experience. During the meeting, I was informed the concession contract for the 55,000-seat stadium was coming up for public bid, and the contract winner would receive a three-year term to supply the concessions with hot dogs, soft drinks, peanuts, and other snacks. Because of my lack of credentials, I enlisted my uncle, who owned Knights Diner in Seattle, as my partner and we bid on the contract. Six weeks later, we were awarded the concessions for Husky Stadium.

At the start of the 1961 football season, we formed Volume Service Company as the corporate entity to operate the concession business. Before the games, I, along with my wife, Joan, and some friends, spent Friday nights bagging peanuts by hand, which we then loaded in the back of a pickup truck. We also installed a speedy service system to better serve the crowds. Strong sales were important to the stadium because they would receive close to 40 percent of all sales dollars.

"I was twenty-eight years old . . . and awarded the concessions to Husky Stadium."

With the concession business satisfying Husky fans—and the stadium pleased with the money we were making—we bid and won the concession and catering contract for the Seattle Center. We then won the concessions contracts for the Oakland Coliseum in California, where the Oakland Raiders and A's played, Arrowhead Stadium in Kansas City, home of the Chiefs, and several other fields around the country. The concessions business often brought me to southern California, where I noticed highly themed restaurants were becoming very popular.

In 1970, we sold Volume Service Company, and the funds were used to start Restaurants Unlimited.

Starting in 1971, my company, Restaurants Unlimited, Inc., built three old-English theme restaurants: Clinkerdagger, Bickerstaff & Pett's Public House in North Seattle in December 1971; another on the Tacoma waterfront in 1972; and Horatio's on Lake Union in October 1971. This was followed by Simon & Seafort's in Anchorage, Horatio's in Honolulu and San Leandro, California, Kincaid's in Minneapolis, and another Clinkerdagger in Spokane, Washington. Later, Restaurants Unlimited opened restaurants in Washington, D.C., Pittsburgh, Philadelphia, Dallas, St. Paul, Los Angeles, Berkeley, and San Francisco, among others. By the start of the 1980s, Americans were changing from car lovers to food lovers. It was apparent we had to learn to cook.

So, we built a large, fully equipped test kitchen in our Restaurants Unlimited home office, which was behind Seattle's Gas Works Park on Lake Union. Our chefs would often conduct food tastings to introduce and test new menu items. I usually attended. It was here that, over the years, I became aware I had a very good "commercial" taste. I tended to favor bold flavors. And what I liked, most of our guests also liked.

While running the food concessions in Arrowhead Stadium, I made many contacts in Kansas City. One day, one of them called to tell me about a shop selling cinnamon rolls in a local mall. I visited the shop and was impressed enough to make an offer to purchase a franchise, but I was told no. I found being turned down was fortuitous because now we had an opportunity to create our own cinnamon roll concept.

Jerilyn Brusseau, who owned a coffee shop in Edmonds, Washington, and who grew up making cinnamon rolls with her grandmother, agreed to come to our test kitchen and work to create a great cinnamon roll. At the time, we had no idea our mysterious cinnamon roll project would ultimately become a national brand with 1,200 franchised locations in 48 countries.

Working five days a week, Jerilyn would bake three or four batches of cinnamon rolls every day. And every day she and I, and later my son Greg, would plan our next experimental batch. For three months, she'd roll out the dough and layer it with a mix of brown sugar, cinnamon, and other ingredients. We brought in proofing ovens and a 20-quart mixer. We hung a sign above the oven emblazoned with just one word, in letters eight inches high: "Irresistible."

We hung a sign above the oven emblazoned with just one word, in letters eight inches high: "Irresistible."

After a month of tasting, we finally developed the pillowy dough. It wasn't cakey or delicate or tough. It was moist and slightly chewy. Then came a major breakthrough. Our Crescent Seasons salesman brought us some unusual cinnamon one day. Up to this point, we were using an average cinnamon. He pointed out that cinnamon isn't just cinnamon. Like wine or coffee, there are different varieties, and cinnamons from different regions, even different elevations, yield their own distinct flavors. After trying different cinnamons from around the world, we settled on Korintje cinnamon, harvested from the bark of the *Cinnamomum burmannii* tree that grows in Indonesia. It delivers cinnamon's familiar punch, but tends toward the sweet and amiable, rather than that devilish bite that punctuates Red Hots candy or schnapps. Suddenly, we were close to our "irresistible" goal.

After two months spent perfecting the flavor and texture, we now struggled with the final baking of the roll. As we applied the layer of the cinnamon-sugar mixture, which melded into a sticky-sweet syrup that we called goo, we saw it kept melting and spilling out from the spiral folds of the dough. The problem was, the dough, which "poofed" up nicely, would slowly shrink during baking, causing the goo to ooze out and puddle at the bottom of our custom-size baking pans we had commissioned for this ambitious endeavor. Earlier, my son Greg, who was out of college now and a manager at our Cutter's restaurant in Seattle, joined us as part of the testing team. He made a final critical adjustment. Instead of pulling the rolls from the oven when they hit an internal temperature of 190°F—typical for a cinnamon roll, which trained bakers use as their guide—he pulled the rolls out at 165°F. He found this to be the ideal temperature because it kept the rolls slightly doughy in the middle while holding the "goo" inside. We described it as "medium rare." And it was that medium-rare consistency, along with the Korintje cinnamon, that made our cinnamon rolls "irresistible."

Our first Cinnabon opened in a mall south of the Seattle airport. Branding genius Terry Heckler presented us with the name Cinnabon. He also happened to be the gentleman responsible for naming another Seattle company: Starbucks.

Soon, all the twenty-two Cinnabons we opened the following year were located inside shopping malls. It was here where customers spent money, hung out, and could watch our rolls being made by hand after they were drawn in by the delicious sights and smells. This network of bakeries provided a new franchise arm for Restaurants Unlimited. By 1990, we had seventy-two Cinnabons scattered throughout the nation. We also opened another restaurant in Seattle, called Palomino—a Mediterranean-style restaurant featuring wood-fired rotisseries and a menu borrowing from Greek, Italian, and other southern European cooking. When we

"At the end of 1990, we had over thirty restaurants along with our Cinnabons."

sold Restaurants Unlimited at the end of 1990, we had over thirty restaurants along with our Cinnabons.

After leaving RUI, I purchased a home on San Juan Island. I remember reading in the *San Juan Journal* about Roche Harbor. The historic and celebrated seaside resort, once owned and operated by lime tycoon John S. McMillin, was involved in bankruptcy and was up for sale. Verne Howard, a resident of San Juan Island, who operated two large grocery stores in town, purchased Roche and later brought me in as a partner. We spent years restoring the famous hotel, building a world-class marina, and fine-tuning the on-property restaurants, and other services. Today, my family and I remain a 50 percent owner of Roche and our partner is the Mike and Lynn Garvey family. I also found cooking as a hobby. Previously, my wife had done all

the cooking. But shortly after she passed, I found cooking to be a fun part of my day—and an interesting hobby.

I'd read recipes in newspapers, magazines, online, and from various blogs. I'd find what interests me and I'd try those recipes, which I would sometimes modify to my liking. My home became my new test kitchen. I'd attempt, on average, three recipes a week. Occasionally, when I'd discover a particular recipe I thought was especially good, I'd file those in a drawer to make again another day. Today, that file consists of more than 120 great-tasting recipes I've accumulated and refined over the years. That's when a lightbulb went off in my head. Imagine if every home cook could experience these recipes.

I discussed the idea with James O. Fraioli, a James Beard Award–winning author from Seattle who runs a boutique publishing company called Culinary Book Creations. He specializes in award-winning cookbooks. We first had the pleasure of working together in 2018, when we teamed up to write *Roche: A Culinary Journey Through San Juan Island's Illustrious Harbor* with Chef Bill Shaw.

James agreed with me that home cooks could benefit from an all-star lineup of excellent and proven five-star recipes. The dishes were retested by local caterer Renee Beachem and others. We narrowed the list to 100, and James helped me to assemble this book. We are delighted to introduce you to *Five-Star Comfort Food*.

I hope you will love and enjoy this cookbook. It's filled with all the delicious kinds of food we know and love, with some great surprises here and there. I love making every recipe, and I hope they will become a regular part of your household, just like they have in mine.

—Rich Komen

> Today, that file consists of more than 120 great-tasting recipes I've accumulated and refined over the years. That's when a lightbulb went off in my head. Imagine if every home cook could experience these recipes.

FIVE-STAR

Dungeness Crab & Artichoke Dip 10

Fredda's Awesome Shrimp de Gallo 12

Fried Pickles with Spicy Mayo 14

Lavender Honey Shrimp 16

Mediterranean Mussels on the Half Shell 20

Prime Beef Poke 22

Shannon's Stuffed Mushrooms 24

Stuffed Tiny Potatoes 26

PASS THE APPETIZERS, PLEASE

DUNGENESS CRAB & ARTICHOKE DIP

½ cup fresh Dungeness crabmeat, drained

½ cup artichoke hearts (unmarinated) coarsely chopped into ½-inch pieces

¼ cup Parmigiano-Reggiano cheese, shredded

¼ cup yellow onion, peeled, cut into quarter sections, then sliced paper thin

1 cup Best Foods or Hellmann's Real Mayonnaise

Italian flat leaf parsley and lemon slice, for garnish

My first encounter with this decadent crab and artichoke dip occurred in the early 1960s while having Christmas dinner at the home of my fiancée, Joan. Her mother, Lou, was an excellent cook, and when I tasted her rich and creamy crab dip, it was love at first sight. Later, Joan perfected the recipe, and the dip appeared on the opening menu of Horatio's and Clinkerdagger, Bickerstaff & Pett's Public in 1971. The crab dip was an instant success and has inspired restaurants in the Northwest to create their own version of this timeless recipe. The common mistakes that cooks make when preparing crab dip are to add additional crab or use a mayonnaise not made with egg yolks. Eggs are an amazing ingredient and are essential to this recipe because, when baked, the crab and mayonnaise make a savory custard-like spread. Adding additional crab or other ingredients will change the egg-to-ingredient ratio resulting in an oily disappointment. Also, make sure you always use Best Foods or Hellmann's for this recipe. The ingredients are real and simple, with eggs, oil, and vinegar.

In a medium bowl, add the Dungeness crab, artichoke hearts, Parmigiano-Reggiano cheese, yellow onion, and mayonnaise. Mix well until combined. Cover with plastic wrap and place in the refrigerator until needed.

Preheat the oven to 400°F.

Before serving, add the desired amount of crab mixture to a heatproof ramekin and place in the oven until an internal temperature of 140°F is achieved, or the mixture is browned on top and bubbling.

Remove from oven and top with fresh parsley and a lemon slice.

Serve with warm, sliced French bread.

FREDDA'S AWESOME SHRIMP DE GALLO

1 pound cooked large shrimp, tails and veins removed, chopped

½ red onion, peeled and diced (about 1 cup)

2 garden tomatoes, diced (about 2 cups)

½ cup pitted black olives, chopped

2 jalapeño peppers seeded and minced

2 limes, juiced (4 tablespoons), or as needed

2 medium avocados, peeled, pitted, and chopped

¼ teaspoon sea salt or as needed

2 cups chopped fresh cilantro leaves, stems removed

Fredda Goldfarb is a close friend of my daughter-in-law, Shannon. Fredda and her husband Steven are also regular guests at our home in Roche Harbor. During our gatherings, Fredda seems to always surprise us with her incredible Shrimp de Gallo, which quickly disappears and is replaced with satisfying smiles. This recipe uses the same fresh ingredients you'd find in authentic pico de gallo—ripe red tomatoes, onion, jalapeño, cilantro, lime, and salt—but then succulent shrimp are added along with olives and avocado for an elevated salsa-based dip. The key to Fredda's pico de gallo is letting it rest. Combine all the ingredients (except the avocado), cover, and refrigerate for a day. The tomatoes will juice up and the flavors will meld. Because the avocado will brown if the dip sits too long, leave out the avocado and add it in just before serving with fresh, crisp tortilla chips.

In a large bowl, add the prawns, onion, tomatoes, olives, and jalapeños. Gently toss to combine then add some of the lime juice along with the avocado, salt, and cilantro. Gently toss again. Add additional lime juice and/or salt to your liking. Place in the refrigerator to chill. Serve chilled with tortilla chips.

2 cups grapeseed or vegetable oil

¾ cup all-purpose flour

2 teaspoons cornstarch

1 teaspoon baking powder

1 cup soda water

3 cucumber pickles, cut into ¼-inch rounds and patted dry

SPICY MAYO

½ cup Best Foods or Hellmann's Real Mayonnaise

1½ teaspoons sriracha

1 teaspoon fresh lemon juice

½ clove garlic, peeled and mashed to a paste

Kosher salt, as needed

FRIED PICKLES WITH SPICY MAYO

It seems just about every food since the 30th century BC (the birth of cooking oil) has been deep-fried. Some successful. Others, not so much. Sliced and coated with a light crip batter, these fried pickles are perfect as an appetizer or fun side dish. While you can certainly make your own pickles, it's much easier to use a favorite store-bought variety. Vlasic's kosher dills, which are fresh, crisp, and crunchy, are a great choice and perfect for dipping in the spicy mayo, which features sriracha, lemon, and garlic. You can use Boar's Head or Claussen kosher dills too.

In a medium heavy saucepan over medium heat, add the grapeseed oil. Heat the oil until 350°F. Note: Use a deep-fry or candy thermometer to achieve the correct temperature.

While the oil is heating, in a medium bowl whisk together the flour, cornstarch, and baking powder. Then slowly whisk in the soda water, a little at a time. The mixture should be the consistency of heavy cream. Use more or less soda water to achieve the correct consistency.

Working in batches, coat the pickle slices with batter, letting the excess drip off. Then carefully add the battered pickles to the hot oil one by one. Note: Adding them individually will prevent the pickles from sticking together. Fry, turning halfway through, until golden brown and crisp on both sides, about 3 minutes per batch.

Using a slotted spoon, transfer the pickles to a paper-lined plate. Serve warm with the Spicy Mayo.

SPICY MAYO

In a small bowl, whisk together the mayonnaise, sriracha, lemon juice, and garlic paste. Season to taste with kosher salt. Set aside until ready to use.

LAVENDER HONEY SHRIMP

16 (16/20 or 21/25) peeled and deveined fresh shrimp with tails on

¼ cup Shrimp Marinade, recipe follows

Vegetable oil, as needed, for frying

1½ cups Tempura Batter, recipe follows

2 lemon wedges, for garnish

¼ cup Honey Sauce, recipe follows

OPTIONAL GARNISHES

¼ cup microgreens

2 to 4 radicchio leaves

2 tablespoons fresh pea sprouts

2 tablespoons shaved daikon radish and/or carrot

2 tablespoons candied macadamia nuts

This mouthwatering dish is from Ko Restaurant in Wailea, Maui. The shrimp get elevated to the next level with a delicious honey glaze but are perfectly delectable on their own. The batter is light and crisp, and if the shrimp are cooked just right, the result is a crunchy appetizer you'll appreciate and enjoy time and time again.

Begin by making the Shrimp Marinade and marinate the shrimp and coat with the cornstarch per the instructions below.

Heat vegetable oil in a deep-sided pot or deep fryer until the oil temperature reaches 350°F.

Dredge the shrimp, holding them by their tails, in the Tempura Batter and let the excess drip off. Carefully place into the hot oil. Deep fry until the shrimp are golden and cooked through, 2 to 3 minutes. Note: Cook in batches if necessary to not over-crowd the deep-frying vessel, which will also lower the temperature of the cooking oil. Remove the shrimp with a slotted spoon and drain on paper towels.

To service, place the microgreens, if desired, in the center of a serving platter. Place the radicchio leaves, if desired, on top and then arrange the shrimp inside and around the leaves. Garnish the perimeter of the plate, if desired, with the pea sprouts, daikon radish and/or carrot, candied macadamia nuts, and lemon slices. Finish with a drizzle of the Honey Sauce over the shrimp and serve immediately.

Continued . . .

SHRIMP MARINADE

1 teaspoon kosher salt

2 teaspoons Chinese wine (or mirin)

2 teaspoons sesame oil

1 egg white

Cornstarch, as needed

TEMPURA BATTER

¾ cup all-purpose flour

½ cup cornstarch

½ tablespoon baking powder

¾ teaspoon kosher salt

¾ cup cold water (more or less)

HONEY SAUCE

¼ cup lavender honey (or regular honey)

2 tablespoons sweetened condensed milk

½ cup Best Foods Real Mayonnaise or Hellmann's Original Mayonnaise

1 tablespoon fresh lemon juice

SHRIMP MARINADE

In a medium-sized bowl, add the salt, wine, sesame oil, and egg white. Whisk until frothy and combined. Add the shrimp and toss well to coat. Place in the refrigerator and let marinate for at least 30 minutes. Remove from refrigerator and drain the shrimp from the marinade. Dredge the shrimp in cornstarch, dusting off the excess. Place the shrimp on wax paper in a single layer and refrigerate for 20 minutes, or until the cornstarch is moist.

TEMPURA BATTER

In a mixing bowl, add the flour, cornstarch, baking powder, and salt. Whisk until well combined. Gradually add the water, a little at a time, until a light, thin batter forms. Set aside until ready to use.

HONEY SAUCE

In a mixing bowl, add the honey, milk, mayonnaise, and lemon juice. Whisk well until combined. Set aside until ready to use.

Shrimp are categorized by weight—specifically, how many pieces make up one pound.

16/20, for example, means 16 to 20 shrimp make up one pound.

8/10 would be considered colossal shrimp, 10/12 would be jumbo, 16/20 would be large, 21/25 would be medium, and 26/30 would be small.

1¼ cups dry white wine

1½ pounds (about 30 to 35) live Mediterranean mussels, scrubbed and debearded

1 hard-boiled egg, halved and pushed through a medium mesh sieve

3 tablespoons white wine vinegar

½ cup finely chopped onion

2 teaspoons small capers, drained and rinsed

1 teaspoon Dijon mustard

1 teaspoon finely chopped fresh Italian flat leaf parsley

1 teaspoon finely chopped fresh chives

1 teaspoon finely chopped fresh chervil

¼ cup olive oil

¼ teaspoon sea salt

¼ teaspoon fresh cracked black pepper

MEDITERRANEAN MUSSELS ON THE HALF SHELL

Cooking fresh mussels only takes minutes and doesn't require any special equipment. Use live Mediterranean mussels. They're large, meaty, and plump. When shopping for mussels, look for unbroken shells that are glossy and rich in color. The mussel should have a clean and salty scent reminiscent of seawater. When you get the mussels home, rinse them in cool water, lightly brush them to remove any sand or grit, and remove the hairy beard that sticks out of the shell. Now they're ready to cook.

In a heavy (5- to 6-quart) pot over medium-high heat, add the wine. When the wine begins to bubble, add the mussels and cover the pot with a lid. Allow the mussels to open. As soon as they open, remove, and transfer them to a shallow baking dish to cool. Keep checking the pot for opened mussels. Discard any closed mussels after 8 minutes.

When the mussels are cool enough to handle, carefully detach the meat and discard half of the shell. Set aside.

In a small bowl, add the minced egg, vinegar, onion, capers, mustard, parsley, chives, and chervil. Whisk well to combine, then slowly add the olive oil while whisking until fully combined. Season to taste with salt and pepper.

Add the mussels to the marinade and gently toss to coat. Cover the bowl and place in the refrigerator for at least 1 hour and up to 6 hours to chill.

Remove the mussels and arrange one mussel in each reserved shell and transfer to a serving platter. Spoon a little of the chilled marinade over the top of each mussel and serve.

1 tablespoon minced garlic

½ tablespoon chopped fresh Italian flat leaf parsley

¼ teaspoon red pepper flakes

1¼ teaspoon sea salt

1 tablespoon Sugar In the Raw turbinado sugar

1 (4-ounce) prime boneless New York (or beef tenderloin) steak, trimmed of fat

¼ cup finely diced sweet onion

¼ cup diced tomato

¼ cup finely diced Japanese or English cucumber

1½ tablespoons sesame oil

¾ teaspoon chili paste (sambal oelek)

PRIME BEEF POKE

Here's another stunning appetizer from Ko Restaurant in Maui that's a meaty twist on the Hawaiian classic, which is normally made from fresh raw fish. Searing the seasoned beef gives this dish a wonderfully intense flavor, with the red pepper flakes and chili paste offering a hit of heat. For the chili paste, use sambal oelek, which is an Indonesian chili paste available at most markets. You can also use Vietnamese or Korean chili paste.

Begin by making the steak rub. In a small bowl, add the garlic, parsley, red pepper flakes, salt, and sugar. Mix well to combine. Then rub the mixture into the steak, making sure to massage well into the meat. Set aside.

To make the accompanying vegetable relish, in another bowl, add the onion, tomato, cucumber, sesame oil, and chili paste. Mix well to combine.

Heat an outdoor or gas grill to high heat or use a sauté pan over high heat on the stove. When ready, add the steak and sear to either medium rare or rare. Remove from the heat and let rest for 10 minutes. Then cut the steak into no larger than ½-inch cubes.

Add the seared steak cubes to a serving bowl and add the vegetable relish. Toss well to coat. Season with additional sea salt, if necessary, and serve immediately.

20 button mushrooms, cleaned with stems removed

Melted butter, as needed, for brushing

1 cup Best Foods or Hellmann's Real Mayonnaise

2 cups grated fresh Parmigiano-Reggiano cheese

1 tablespoon fresh lemon juice

1 cup minced, cooked (stiff but not crisp) bacon (10 to 12 slices of center cut naturally smoked bacon)

⅓ cup minced fresh scallion

SHANNON'S STUFFED MUSHROOMS

You gotta try these stuffed mushrooms from my daughter-in-law, Shannon. They're fun and delicious with a combination of smoked bacon, scallion, and grated Parmesan cheese with a bit of citrus. They're also versatile; fancy enough for a special occasion or holiday party, but simple enough to add to a weeknight family dinner. Like many other recipes in this book, use Best Foods or Hellmann's Real Mayonnaise when called for. Also make sure the stuffing mixture doesn't get too watery. Go light on the lemon juice as you can always add more juice to thin the mixture if necessary.

Using a paring knife, enlarge the stem hole of each mushroom if you prefer a larger cavity to add more filling. Then brush the mushrooms with melted butter. Arrange the mushrooms stem-side up on a foil-lined baking sheet.

In a large mixing bowl, add the mayonnaise, cheese, lemon juice, bacon, and scallion. Mix well until combined. Then stuff each mushroom cavity with the mixture and mound the stuffing on top, about ½ inch high. Refrigerate until ready to serve, or heat immediately.

To heat, preheat the oven to broil and place the top rack about 6 inches from the heating element.

Place the tray of mushrooms under the broiler. Broil until the mushrooms are browned (but not charred) and the stuffing is bubbling, about 2½ minutes. Remove from the oven and let cool slightly before serving.

1 pound (about 18) small new potatoes (about 1½ to 2 inches), washed and dried

¼ cup Best Foods or Hellmann's Real Mayonnaise

¼ cup grated Asiago cheese

Finely minced fresh scallion, as needed, for garnish

STUFFED TINY POTATOES

This easy appetizer features sweet, moist, thin-skinned new potatoes that are fresh in late summer and early fall. If you prepare this appetizer when new potatoes are not in season, you can easily substitute small red-skin potatoes. The flavor of the Asiago cheese blends well with Best Foods or Hellmann's Real Mayonnaise, resulting in a cheesy-mayo mixture that will not be soggy.

Bring a pot of salted water to a boil. Add the potatoes and cook until fork-tender, being careful not to overcook the potatoes, about 10 minutes. Remove the potatoes and let cool to the touch.

Meanwhile, in a mixing bowl, add the mayonnaise and cheese and mix until well combined.

Set the oven to broil and place a rack just beneath the heating element.

When the potatoes are ready to handle, gently slice each potato in half lengthwise, being careful not to tear the skins when cutting. Then cut a thin slice from the bottom so they will stand. Using a melon baller or small spoon, scoop out a large indentation in each potato half and discard. Then fill each indentation with the cheese mixture.

Arrange the potato halves on a sheet tray. Transfer the potatoes to the oven and broil until nicely brown and slightly crisp. Remove from the oven and garnish each potato half with some finely minced scallion before serving.

FIVE-STAR

★★★★★

Bev's Snappy Seafood Salad 30

Heirloom Tomatoes with Garlicky White Sauce...... 32

Maytag Blue Cheese Salad 34

Picnic Potato Salad...37

Watermelon & Charred Tomato Salad 38

Cream of Mushroom Soup 40

Garden Fresh Tomato Soup 44

Mama Leone's Chicken Soup 46

Split Pea Soup with Ham 48

Corn-Cheddar Chowder...49

SALADS,
SOUPS &
A CHOWDER

BEV'S SNAPPY SEAFOOD SALAD

8 ounces dry angel-hair pasta

2 tablespoons butter

1 pound small uncooked fresh or frozen shrimp, peeled and deveined

Salt and fresh cracked black pepper, as needed, to season

¼ cup fresh lemon juice

1 bunch (about ½ cup) scallions, finely minced

1½ cups finely minced celery

¾ cup Best Foods or Hellmann's Real Mayonnaise

½ cup Wishbone Italian Dressing

1 lime, zested

1½ cups grated fresh Parmigiano-Reggiano cheese

Accompaniments (as needed): butter lettuce cups, tomato wedges, Parmesan crisps or crisp pita bread halves baked with Parmesan cheese

This salad—a blend of shrimp, lemon, pasta, and cheese with Italian dressing that is served chilled in crisp lettuce cups—is one of the more interesting recipes I've enjoyed. Take one bite and at first you might think nothing of it, but by the third bite you'll discover it's addictive. To perfect this recipe, use 25/30 or 30/35 frozen shrimp (as 16/20 get expensive and are easy to overcook). Make sure the shrimp are briefly sautéed to medium or medium rare. You want a crunch to the bite. Also, chop the shrimp into small bite-size pieces. This will help when blending the shrimp with the pasta. Same with the vegetables. Finely mince the onion and celery, which you can accomplish using a food processor. Just don't over mince or you'll get mush; a few pulses, scraping down the sides, and mixing again with several more pulses should do the trick. If it doesn't work the first time, start over and try again.

Cook the pasta in salted boiling water until al dente or desired consistency, about 3 minutes. Drain well, rinse in cold water until cool, and drain again. Set aside.

In a large sauté pan, melt the butter over medium-high heat. When hot, add the shrimp and sauté until medium rare so they are crunchy to the bite, 2 to 3 minutes. Remove from heat and season the shrimp with salt and pepper. Chop the shrimp into small bite-size pieces.

In a large bowl, add the cooked shrimp, lemon juice, scallion, celery, mayonnaise, Italian dressing, lime zest, and cooked pasta. Toss well to combine, then fold in the grated cheese. Place in the refrigerator for several hours or for a day.

Spoon the salad in butter lettuce cups and garnish with tomato wedges, Parmesan crisps or crisp pita bread halves baked with Parmesan cheese.

HEIRLOOM TOMATOES WITH GARLICKY WHITE SAUCE

1 cup Best Foods or Hellmann's Real Mayonnaise

½ cup evaporated milk

1 garlic clove, peeled and minced

1 large pinch kosher salt, plus more for seasoning the tomatoes

3 grinds of fresh cracked black pepper, plus more for seasoning the tomatoes

3 pounds mixed heirloom tomatoes, sliced into rounds or cut into wedges or bite-sized chunks

1 tablespoon dried oregano leaves

If you have fresh tomatoes from the garden, like I do, they're perfect for this recipe. Tomatoes are best during the summer months when it's peak tomato season and I'm picking homegrown tomatoes fresh off the vine. Of course, you can use any kind of tomatoes so long as they're fresh and ripe. Try to avoid store-bought tomatoes unless they're heirloom. That's because most tomatoes found in supermarkets are grown for storage and shipping, not for taste. You can also try cherry or grape tomatoes, sliced in half, which often taste better than the usual larger supermarket variety.

In a bowl, add the mayonnaise, evaporated milk, garlic, large pinch of salt, and 3 grinds of the black pepper. Whisk until well combined (should be the consistency of thin pancake batter). Cover and keep refrigerated until ready to serve. Note: This Garlicky White Sauce can be made the day ahead. Makes 1¾ cups.

In a large bowl, add the tomatoes and a large pinch of salt. Gently toss then arrange on a serving platter. Drizzle the Garlicky White Sauce over the tomatoes to your liking. Finish with another grind or two of pepper, and sprinkle with oregano before serving.

3 romaine hearts

1 cup Maytag Blue Cheese Dressing, recipe follows

2 eggs

2 tablespoons slivered almonds

4 tablespoons Maytag blue cheese

Fresh cracked black pepper

MAYTAG BLUE CHEESE SALAD

The Maytag Blue Cheese Salad was a longtime favorite at Restaurants Unlimited's Palomino and Kincaid's restaurants. Chef Bill Shaw, now at Roche Harbor, improved this recipe over the years. Today, it's served at Roche Harbor Resort, and has been our most popular salad for more than twenty-five years, thanks to the amazing cheese, which is always among the top 100 cheeses in the world. When we suggest this salad to new guests of Roche, some tell us right away they do not care for blue cheese. However, after their first bite of this ripened cheese, they're often hooked. The dressing, meanwhile, adds the perfect creaminess to the crisp romaine. It also makes a wonderful dip for vegetables and adds a new flavor to your favorite hot wing recipe. You can get Maytag and other excellent, creamy blue cheese at Maytag Dairy Farms, Point Reyes Farmstead Cheese Co., and Rogue Creamery.

Remove the outer dark green leaves from the romaine head until only the light green leaves are exposed. Then cut away the soft dark green tops. Slice the romaine heart in half lengthwise then slice the romaine by placing the heart cut-side down on a cutting board and run your knife lengthwise from the stem to the tip, creating three 1½-inch strips. Next, slice the strips into 1½-inch-square pieces. Soak the chopped romaine in a bowl of ice-cold water for 20 minutes. This will allow the romaine to absorb the moisture, resulting in a crispier bite. Drain the water and dry the romaine on a towel or in a lettuce spinner. Place the lettuce in the refrigerator with a damp towel covering the lettuce until you are ready to serve.

Boil the eggs by placing them in a saucepan with cold water over medium-high heat. When the water begins to boil, cover the saucepan with a lid and remove from heat. Allow the eggs to slowly cook for 18 minutes. Drain the hot water and place the saucepan in the sink with the eggs. Pour cold water over the eggs until they are cool, about 15 minutes. Crack and peel the eggs in the water. Using a fine cheese grater, grate the eggs into a bowl then refrigerate.

Preheat the oven to 350°F.

Place the slivered almonds on a cookie sheet and bake until light golden brown, stirring the almonds halfway through. Remove the toasted almonds and allow to cool.

Place the blue cheese in the freezer for 15 to 20 minutes. Freezing the cheese makes it easier to slice and crumble. Remove and slice into ¼-inch slices and break apart by hand into ½-inch pieces, then refrigerate.

When ready to serve, pour Maytag Blue Cheese Dressing over the chilled romaine and toss by hand, careful not to bruise the lettuce. After the romaine is coated with the dressing, place equal amounts of dressed romaine on four chilled plates and build the romaine into a volcano shape. The correct amount of dressing gives the salad a rich, creamy, and crisp crunch with each bite. Note: Use a heavy amount of dressing. It's best when the entire salad is "gooey."

Garnish each salad with 1 tablespoon of the grated egg, followed by the toasted almonds and finally the crumbled blue cheese. Allow the egg, almonds, and blue cheese to cascade down the mound of dressed romaine. Serve immediately with fresh cracked pepper and a chilled salad fork.

Maytag Blue Cheese Dressing recipe on page 36

¾ cup (6 ounces) Maytag blue cheese

1 teaspoon peeled and finely chopped fresh garlic

¼ teaspoon dry mustard

½ teaspoon fresh cracked black pepper

½ teaspoon onion powder

¼ teaspoon white pepper

3 tablespoons red wine vinegar

1 teaspoon Worcestershire sauce

3 drops Tabasco hot sauce

¾ cup sour cream

2 cups Best Foods or Hellmann's Real Mayonnaise

⅓ cup buttermilk

MAYTAG BLUE CHEESE DRESSING

Place the blue cheese in the freezer for 15 to 20 minutes. Freezing the cheese makes it easier to slice and crumble. Remove and slice into ¼-inch slices and break apart by hand into ½-inch pieces.

In a medium-sized bowl, add the garlic, dry mustard, black pepper, onion powder, and white pepper. Mix well with a wire whip. Add the vinegar, Worcestershire sauce, and Tabasco. Continue to mix until thoroughly combined. Add the sour cream, mayonnaise, and buttermilk. Mix for 2 minutes, creating a creamy mixture. Add the blue cheese crumbles and gently fold into the creamy mixture, now creating a chunky blue cheese dressing. Transfer to a nonreactive dish (such as stainless steel, ceramic, glass, or metal cookware with an enamel coating) and refrigerate overnight to allow the flavors to blend. Note: The dressing should be just thin enough to flow from a ladle. If the dressing needs to be thinned to the desired consistency, add more buttermilk.

PICNIC
POTATO SALAD

Serves 10

I have tried many versions of potato salad. Most are good, but this one is better. For years, many of my friends and I thought my wife Joanie made the best potato salad. Then one day about eleven years ago, I attended a wedding party in the farming community of Scio, Oregon. I remember a long table filled with many dishes brought by the family, including a large bowl of potato salad, which looked just like Joanie's. It was outstanding. The young lady who made it shared the recipe with me along with how to make it (note: it takes a couple days to make but is well worth it). The secret is diced red onion and a lot more eggs. This really makes the difference. Today, I make this potato salad every Fourth of July for ten to twenty of my closest friends.

Peel the potatoes and cut into quarters. Place the chunks in a large pot of boiling water and cook until the internal temperature of the potatoes reaches 185°F. Note: Overcooking will cause the potatoes to get mushy. Remove the potatoes and immediately cool the potatoes in ice water. When cold, remove the potatoes and reserve in the refrigerator overnight.

The next day, cut the potato chunks into smaller pieces, ½-inch to ⅝-inch squares. Set aside.

Boil the eggs and chill immediately in ice water once boiled. When cold, peel the eggs right away and dice.

In a large mixing bowl, add the potatoes, eggs, onion, mayonnaise, mustard, salt, onion salt, celery salt, white and black pepper. Mix well and reserve in the refrigerator overnight. This will allow the potatoes to absorb much of the salt and flavor. Taste the next day and add, if needed, additional mustard, onion salt, and celery salt. Add some additional mayonnaise too if the mixture is too dry; it should be a "gooey" consistency.

Ingredients

- 2½ pounds russet or white potatoes
- 12 eggs
- ½ medium-sized red onion, peeled and finely diced (about 1 cup)
- ¾ cup Best Foods or Hellmann's Real Mayonnaise
- ¼ cup plus 1 tablespoon yellow mustard
- 1½ teaspoons salt
- 3 teaspoons onion salt
- 1 teaspoon celery salt
- ½ teaspoon white pepper
- ¼ teaspoon fresh cracked black pepper

WATERMELON & CHARRED TOMATO SALAD

6 to 8 plum tomatoes, halved

Extra-virgin olive oil, as needed

2 pounds seedless watermelon, rind removed, flesh cut into ½-inch cubes

1 English cucumber, peeled, seeded, and cut into ½-inch cubes

3 tablespoons fresh lime juice

¼ teaspoon crushed red pepper

½ cup chopped fresh cilantro leaves

Kosher salt, as needed

During the summer months when outdoor grills are in full swing, char some fresh tomatoes for a feel-good salad that goes well with any grilled meat. I love this salad for any barbecue. The combination of blistered tomatoes with watermelon chunks and cucumber results in a "swell" salad. Watermelon and charred tomatoes may seem like an unlikely pairing, but it works.

Prepare and preheat an outdoor or gas grill on high heat.

Brush the tomatoes with the olive oil and place cut-side down on the grill until charred and blistered for about 4 minutes. (Note: Only sear one side of the tomatoes and do not overcook or they will turn mushy.) Remove the tomatoes from the grill and let cool completely. When cool, cut into ½-inch cubes.

In a large bowl, add the charred tomatoes along with the watermelon, cucumber, lime juice, crushed red pepper, and cilantro. Toss gently to combine and season with salt before serving.

CREAM OF MUSHROOM SOUP

3 quarts Mushroom Broth, recipe follows (or use 4 tablespoons Better Than Bouillon Mushroom Base mixed with 3 quarts water)

2½ pounds whole medium-sized cremini mushrooms, cleaned

¾ teaspoon fresh cracked black pepper

¾ teaspoon white pepper

1½ teaspoons mustard powder

1½ teaspoons onion powder

1½ teaspoons garlic powder

2 teaspoons dried dill

1½ teaspoons dried thyme

3 to 5 tablespoons olive oil

5 cups sliced medium-sized mushrooms, divided

1 cup butter

1 cup all-purpose flour

3 cups heavy cream

3 tablespoons Worcestershire sauce

Salt to taste

This full-flavored mushroom soup recipe with tender bites of mushroom pieces is a great favorite of mine. In fact, most people are surprised by the depth of flavor this soup has. This is one of many recipes I rate "better than 5-star." The recipe originated from Anne Gubanc, wife of Tony, founders of Gubanc's Restaurant in Lake Oswego, Oregon, in 1976. They still use forty pounds of mushrooms at the restaurant to get the portions they need. Thankfully this home-friendly version has been reduced and adapted using an easy-to-make mushroom broth for better flavor. For the mushrooms, use cremini. You can also use mini portobello or a combination of your favorite mushroom varieties. For the broth, you can make it from scratch (the recipe follows), or you can use Better Than Bouillon (available at grocery stores or online) or another similar mushroom base.

In a medium-sized soup pot over high heat, add the Mushroom Broth and whole mushrooms, and bring to a boil. Then reduce the heat and simmer partially covered for approximately 2 hours.

Remove the pot from the heat and puree the contents using either an immersion blender or kitchen blender. Note: Use caution when blending hot liquids in a kitchen blender. Best to blend in several batches and always pulse several times before blending the mixture on medium speed until mushrooms are pureed. Store the mixture covered in the refrigerator.

Next, in a small bowl, add the black pepper, white pepper, mustard powder, onion powder, garlic powder, dried dill, and dried thyme. Mix well until combined.

In the bottom of a medium-sized soup pot over medium heat, add the olive oil. When hot, add 2 cups of the sliced mushrooms and the seasoning mixture. Stir the mushrooms and seasonings

off and on for 5 minutes with a whisk until the mushrooms are cooked. Note: If the mushrooms and mixture seem dry, add a little more olive oil. Now add the pureed mushroom mixture to the pot and stir to combine. Continue to cook the mixture over medium heat.

In the meantime, make a roux by melting the butter in a medium saucepan over medium heat. Add the flour and whisk well. Continue to cook the roux for a few minutes then reduce the heat to low. Allowing the roux to slowly cook over medium heat creates a nutty flavor that enhances soups and sauces. Add the heavy cream to the soup pot and bring the soup to just below a boil. Once well heated, add the roux a little at a time to the soup pot and whisk well to incorporate. The soup will thicken as it continues to heat, so add more or less roux depending on the soup consistency you prefer. Make sure the soup does not boil. Next, add the Worcestershire sauce and remaining sliced mushrooms, and continue to cook until the mushrooms are soft. Season with salt if necessary and serve or keep in the refrigerator for several days to serve later.

MUSHROOM BROTH

In a large soup pot over high heat, add the water, mushrooms, dried porcinis, carrots, onions, bay leaves, and garlic. Season with salt and pepper. Bring to a boil, then reduce the heat to low and simmer, partially covered, for 45 minutes. Remove from the heat and double strain. Reserve the broth until ready to use.

3½ quarts water

3 pounds mushrooms, cleaned and chopped; leave some whole

8 dried porcini mushrooms

2 carrots, chopped

2 medium yellow onions, peeled and chopped

2 bay leaves

6 garlic cloves, peeled and chopped

Salt to taste

Fresh cracked black pepper to taste

GARDEN FRESH TOMATO SOUP

5 to 6 cups chopped fresh heirloom tomatoes

1 medium yellow onion, peeled and thinly sliced

4 whole cloves garlic

2 cups chicken broth

3 tablespoons butter

3 tablespoons all-purpose flour

1 teaspoon granulated sugar, or to taste

1 teaspoon salt

Chopped fresh basil leaves, if desired, for garnish

I find the best tomato soup recipe is one that is simple to make and uses fresh ingredients—just like this recipe. It's also light, bright, and appropriate for all seasons. This easy soup can be prepared in under an hour, making it the perfect weeknight meal. I prefer fresh ripe heirloom tomatoes from the garden, but you can use any garden-fresh variety. You've never had tomato soup until you've had it with fresh homegrown tomatoes.

In a stockpot over medium heat, add the tomatoes, onion, cloves, and chicken broth. Stir to combine and bring to a boil. Reduce the heat to medium-low and allow to gently boil for 20 minutes to blend all the flavors. Remove from the heat and push the contents through a food mill or strainer into a large bowl or pan. Discard the leftover sediment and fine particles left behind.

In the same stockpot, melt the butter over medium heat. Stir in the flour to make a roux. Cook until the roux is medium brown. Gradually whisk in the tomato mixture, making sure no lumps are formed. Season, to taste, with sugar and salt and garnish with chopped fresh basil leaves before serving.

2 carrots, coarsely chopped

5 ribs celery, (2 chopped, 3 diced), divided

2 medium yellow onion, peeled (1 chopped, 1 diced), divided

2 bay leaves

4 or 5 sprigs fresh thyme

½ teaspoon fresh cracked black pepper, plus more for seasoning

Salt, as needed

1 (5½ pound) whole chicken

1 tablespoon olive oil

1 tablespoon butter

1 tablespoon minced garlic

½ teaspoon dried tarragon

½ teaspoon dried oregano

2 teaspoons dried thyme

2 teaspoons Hungarian sweet paprika

½ cup plus 2 tablespoons Wondra

2 to 4 cups reserved chicken stock

4 cups store-bought chicken stock (or use 4 teaspoons Better Than Bouillon Roasted Chicken Base mixed with 4 cups water)

1 (15 ounce) can diced tomatoes with juice

¾ cup heavy cream

2 cups chopped fresh spinach

MAMA LEONE'S CHICKEN SOUP

Since 1979, Elephant's Deli in Portland has been making great local foods from scratch. One of those is their classically famous Mama Leone's Chicken Soup. It's chunky but not too chunky, savory, but not too salty, and rich but not too creamy. You'll find a number of versions of this recipe online, but this adaptation tastes much like the original. By slowly cooking the chicken with herbs and vegetables for 6 to 7 hours, the result is a better dish. However, a fresh rotisserie chicken still makes for a terrific soup.

In a slow cooker set on low, add the carrots, 2 ribs of chopped celery, 1 chopped onion, bay leaves, and thyme. Season the chicken with salt and pepper and place on top of the vegetables. Add about 1½ cups of water. This will help create the stock. Cook the chicken and aromatics until the chicken is tender, 6 to 7 hours. Remove the chicken from the slow cooker and let cool to the touch. Remove the meat and cube (or shred) 3 cups of chicken. Reserve the stock (2 to 4 cups).

In a heavy stockpot over medium-low heat, add the oil and butter. When hot, add 1 diced onion and 3 ribs of diced celery, and cook, stirring occasionally, until the onions are translucent, 6 to 7 minutes. Add the garlic, tarragon, oregano, thyme, paprika, and ½ teaspoon of pepper. Cook while stirring, 3 to 4 minutes. Add the Wondra and stir until well combined. Slowly whisk in the reserved and canned chicken stocks. Bring to a boil and add the tomatoes and cream. Reduce the heat to low and simmer, uncovered, for 20 minutes. Add the reserved chicken and simmer for 10 minutes. Just before serving, stir in the spinach.

SPLIT PEA SOUP WITH HAM

¼ cup butter

1 large white or yellow onion, peeled and chopped (2 cups)

1 large carrot, peeled and diced into ¼-inch pieces (1 cup)

1½ large ribs of celery, peeled and diced into ¼-inch pieces (1 cup)

½ teaspoon fresh cracked black pepper

3 cloves garlic, peeled and minced

1 pound dried split peas, rinsed and sorted

2 pounds fully cooked hickory smoked ham shank (or similar ham bone)

1 large bay leaf (or 2 small)

2 teaspoons chopped fresh thyme leaves, divided

½ teaspoon smoked paprika

3 cups chicken stock (use low sodium if ham and bones are pre-salted)

3 cups cold water

½ to 1 cup ham steak, cut into ¼-inch cubes

Garlic and butter-flavored croutons (Texas Toast), as needed for garnish

Split pea soup with ham is a classic, made from split peas that have been hulled, dried, and split, and a pork broth made by simmering a ham bone. For this delicious recipe, I use green split peas, which are sweeter and commonly used in split pea soup recipes as compared to their yellow counterpart. Use a fully cooked smoked ham shank if you can. You can also use any ham bone so long as it's meaty. This recipe is simple to make and hearty enough to serve as a meal.

In a large pot or Dutch oven over medium heat, add the butter. When melted and the foaming subsides, add the onion, carrot, celery, and pepper. Mix well and cook, stirring occasionally, until the vegetables are softened and just beginning to brown, 5 to 8 minutes. Stir in the garlic and cook until aromatic, about 1 minute. Stir in the split peas. Next, add the ham shank (or bone), along with the bay leaf, 1 teaspoon thyme, and smoked paprika. Stir in the chicken stock and water. Bring to a boil, then reduce heat and allow to simmer, uncovered, for 60 to 90 minutes, stirring occasionally. Note: Stir more frequently as the soup begins to thicken; add additional stock and/or water if the consistency gets too thick for your taste. Add the cubed ham during the last 20 minutes of cooking.

When ready to serve, remove and discard the ham shank (bone) and bay leaf. Stir in the remaining thyme leaves and check the seasoning. Add salt and pepper, if needed. Transfer to individual soup bowls and garnish with some garlic and butter-flavored croutons just before serving.

CORN-CHEDDAR CHOWDER

Serves 6

No matter what precedes the word "chowder," one typically envisions a hearty, warm, chunky soup. And this is certainly the case with this simple, yet savory rich Corn-Cheddar Chowder recipe. The pork fat from the bacon lends a rich base and the milk fat from the simmered fresh corncobs pumps up the corn flavor. A full-bodied chicken base is enhanced with heavy cream, milk, sharp white cheddar cheese, and cream cheese. The cooking time for this chowder is less than one hour, and the flavors are wonderful when reheated as leftovers the next day.

In a large pot over medium-high heat, add the bacon and cook, stirring occasionally, until almost crisp. Remove the bacon and reserve on paper towels to drain. When cool, finely chop the bacon, and set aside.

To the drippings in the pot, add the carrot, onion, bell pepper, celery, and garlic. Cook until softened, about 5 minutes. Next, stir in the flour and cook for about 3 minutes. Whisk in the broth and add the potatoes, corncobs, bay leaves, cayenne pepper, and thyme sprigs. Increase the heat to high, bring to a boil, then reduce the heat to medium-low. Simmer the chowder until the potatoes are fork-tender, 10 to 12 minutes. Discard the corncobs, bay leaves, and thyme sprigs. Add half of the reserved bacon bits along with the corn kernels, cream, milk, cheddar cheese, and cream cheese. Simmer until the cheeses have melted and the mixture is smooth. Season with salt and pepper, garnish with the remaining bacon bits and sliced scallions, and serve.

2½ cups finely chopped thick-sliced bacon (7 to 8 strips)

1 cup diced carrot

1 cup diced onion

1 cup diced red bell pepper

1 cup diced celery

1½ tablespoons minced fresh garlic

⅓ cup all-purpose flour

4 cups chicken broth

2½ cups (about 8 ounces) cubed Yukon Gold or red-skinned potatoes

5 ears fresh sweet corn, shucked and kernels removed (about 4 cups), cobs reserved

2 bay leaves

⅛ teaspoon cayenne pepper

2 sprigs fresh thyme

1½ cups heavy cream

½ cup whole milk

½ cup (about 4½ ounces) shredded sharp white cheddar cheese

¼ cup (about 2 ounces) cubed softened cream cheese

Salt, as needed

Fresh cracked black pepper, as needed

Sliced scallions, as needed, for garnish

FIVE-STAR

Best Tuna Noodle Casserole 52

Bev & Joanie's Famous Baked Spaghetti 54

Dungeness Crab Pot Macaroni & Cheese 58

Classic Clam Linguine 61

Pappardelle with Chicken Ragù, Fennel & Peas 62

Pasta Puttanesca 66

Tagliatelle Bolognese 68

Pork Lo Mein 72

PASTA & NOODLE BOWLS

BEST TUNA NOODLE CASSEROLE

2 tablespoons butter, divided

½ cup diced yellow onion

½ cup diced celery

1 cup thinly sliced mushrooms

1 (10.5-ounce) can cream of chicken soup

½ cup Best Foods or Hellmann's Real Mayonnaise

¼ cup whole milk

½ cup heavy cream

¼ cup sour cream

2 teaspoons dry sherry

1½ teaspoons Dijon mustard

⅛ teaspoon nutmeg

1 teaspoon Worcestershire sauce

½ cup frozen petite peas

2 hard-boiled eggs, shelled and chopped

1 large (12 ounce) can solid white albacore tuna packed in water, squeeze-drained

8 ounces cooked egg noodles

¾ cup shredded sharp cheddar cheese

¼ teaspoon fresh cracked black pepper

Although most associated with 1950s Middle America, the iconic tuna noodle casserole first appeared in Sunset Magazine in 1930, the recipe titled: Noodles and Tuna Fish en Casserole. Today, the recipe hasn't changed much—canned tuna and egg noodles are smothered in a creamy filling with cheese and peas. Campbell's Soup refers to this classic meal as the "original dump-and-bake dinner, always ready to go right from your pantry." Growing up, my mother relied on tuna casserole to keep our family fed. As a cook who can afford better ingredients, I like this elevated version of the vintage casserole.

Preheat the oven to 375°F.

In a medium sauté pan over medium heat, add 1 tablespoon of the butter. When melted, add the onion and celery and sauté. As the vegetables begin to soften, add the mushrooms, and cook until slightly softened, 2 to 3 minutes. Note: If the mushrooms get too soft, they'll shrink away during baking. Remove the vegetables and mushrooms from the pan and let cool.

In a large bowl, add the cream of chicken soup, mayonnaise, milk, heavy cream, and sour cream. Mix well until combined. Then add the sherry, mustard, nutmeg, and Worcestershire sauce. Mix well until combined. Next, fold in the sautéed vegetables and mushrooms along with the peas, hard-boiled eggs, tuna, noodles, and cheese. Season with black pepper and pour the creamy mixture into a buttered casserole dish. Cover with foil and bake in the preheated oven for 12 minutes. Remove the foil and continue to bake for 20 minutes or until the internal temperature of the casserole reaches 175°F to 180°F, about 30 minutes. Note: Check the temperature after 20 minutes, and make sure the temperature does not exceed 180°F.

Remove from the oven and let cool slightly before serving.

Visit the fish grocery aisle, and you'll see cans labeled white, light, or chunk light tuna. What's the difference?

White: This refers to albacore tuna.

Light: This label can include a variety of tuna species; often skipjack, but may also be a mix of skipjack, yellowfin, bigeye, or tongol.

Chunk light: This indicates light tuna in smaller pieces, instead of a packed fillet.

BEV & JOANIE'S FAMOUS BAKED SPAGHETTI

SAUCE

1 pound ground round beef

6 sprigs fresh Italian flat leaf parsley, minced (about 3 tablespoons)

4 cloves garlic, peeled and minced

1 pound ground Italian sausage (½ mild & ½ hot, or vary the amount to your desired spice level)

2 tablespoons olive oil

2 medium yellow onions, peeled and minced

1 medium green bell pepper, cored, seeded, and minced

2 ribs celery, minced

1½ cups cremini mushrooms, cleaned and sliced

1 (6 ounce) can tomato paste

1 (14.5 ounce) can chopped tomatoes

1 (29 ounce) can tomato sauce

1 cup tomato juice

1 cup water

1 stick (½ cup) butter

1 teaspoon beef bouillon

1 teaspoon dried basil

Continued . . .

Hands down, this is my favorite recipe. Simply toss the pasta with the sauce, pour into an ovenproof dish, and bake. It's that easy. This dish also freezes extremely well. If you like your sauce spicy, you can use more hot Italian sausage. When cooking, I like the sausage and ground beef broken up fine so they permeate the pasta. To help break them up, I'll use a dough cutter while the meat is cooking. This seems to work well. For the minced onion, bell pepper, and celery, this can be prepared in two batches in a food processor. Be careful not to process too much or it will turn to mush. You want a nice mince. Typically, I make a batch of this sauce, which is about 13 cups, to store in 2-cup plastic containers in the freezer. The other day, I found a container in the freezer from two and a half years ago. I thawed, reheated, and tried the pasta. It was excellent; another one of those "better than five-star" recipes. I don't recommend storing the sauce for that long, but it was still delicious.

In a large sauté pan over medium heat, add the ground beef, parsley, and garlic. Finely crumble and cook the beef until browned, about 3 to 4 minutes. Remove from heat, drain the beef, and transfer to large stockpot. Replace the sauté pan over medium heat and add the sausage. Cook until browned and broken into a small crumble, about 6 to 7 minutes. Transfer the sausage (do not drain) to the stockpot. Replace the sauté pan over medium heat and add the olive oil. When hot, add the minced onion, bell pepper, and celery. Cook, stirring occasionally, until soft, about 5 to 6 minutes. Transfer to the stockpot along with the sliced raw mushrooms. Then stir in the tomato paste, chopped tomatoes (with liquid), tomato sauce, tomato

1 teaspoon minced fresh rosemary

1½ tablespoons Kitchen Bouquet Browning & Seasoning Sauce

1½ teaspoons fresh cracked black pepper

2 teaspoons to 1 tablespoon granulated sugar, or as needed, to taste

2 teaspoons to 1 tablespoon salt, or as needed, to taste

PASTA

Thin spaghetti, as needed (for 1 pound of cooked pasta, use 5 cups of sauce; or 2½ ounces of sauce for every 1 ounce of dried thin spaghetti)

juice, water, butter, beef bouillon, basil, rosemary, browning and seasoning sauce, and black pepper. Stir in the sugar and salt, if at all, to taste. Depending on the acidity of the tomatoes, you may need more or less sugar, and salt. Place the stockpot on a low simmer and cover with the lid cracked slightly. Simmer for 1½ to 2 hours, stirring occasionally. Remove from the heat and set aside.

Preheat the oven to 350°F.

Boil the spaghetti in a large pot of salted water until al dente (the pasta will continue to cook while baking in the oven). Drain the pasta well and add to a large bowl and toss with the sauce, using the ratio noted under "Pasta" above.

Transfer the pasta and sauce into a greased ovenproof baking dish. Cover with aluminum foil and place in the preheated oven for 15 minutes. Remove the foil and continue to bake for 25 minutes. Removing the foil will allow the pasta to dry out a bit, which improves the texture.

DUNGENESS CRAB POT MACARONI & CHEESE

¾ cup Japanese-style panko breadcrumbs

3 tablespoons grated fresh Parmigiano-Reggiano cheese

1 tablespoon finely chopped fresh Italian flat leaf parsley

1 teaspoon peeled and minced fresh garlic

3 tablespoons butter, melted

4 cups Garlic Cream Sauce, recipe follows

1 cup grated cheddar cheese

¼ cup grated fresh Parmigiano-Reggiano cheese

4 cups ziti pasta, cooked al dente

½ pound fresh Dungeness crabmeat

1 cup Au Gratin Topping, recipe follows

Inside the busy sauté station at Roche Harbor Resort's fast-paced Madrona Bar & Grill, Chef Bill Shaw serves up one of our summer hits—crab mac and cheese. Creamy, cheesy, and loaded with fresh, local Dungeness crab, it's fun to elevate comfort classics like this one. When making the mac and cheese, we prefer using ziti. Its shape goes best with chunky ingredients that can get trapped in the hollow centers. If you don't have ziti on hand, any medium-sized tubular pasta shape will work.

In a mixing bowl, combine the breadcrumbs, Parmigiano-Reggiano cheese, parsley, and garlic. Slowly drizzle the melted butter into the mixture while stirring. Continue to stir until the butter is evenly distributed and absorbed by the breadcrumbs. Set aside.

Preheat the oven to 350°F.

In a large nonstick saucepan over medium heat, add the Garlic Cream Sauce, cheddar cheese, and ¼ cup Parmigiano-Reggiano cheese. When the sauce begins to bubble, add the cooked pasta and continue cooking until the pasta is warm. Place the heated pasta and cheese in a baking dish. Sprinkle the Dungeness crabmeat over the top of the pasta followed by the breadcrumb mixture, allowing the crab to peek through. Place in the oven and bake until the top is golden-brown, and the center of the pasta is hot.

Garlic Cream Sauce recipe on page 60

½ cup butter

¼ cup olive oil

4 garlic cloves, peeled and minced

4 cups heavy cream

1 teaspoon kosher salt

2 teaspoons freshly cracked black pepper

GARLIC CREAM SAUCE

Note: It is best to use a heavy-gauge saucepan to avoid scalding the cream.

Heat the butter and olive oil in a saucepan over medium heat until the butter is melted. Add the garlic and reduce heat to low. Simmer for 5 to 8 minutes, or until the garlic softens. Note: Do not allow garlic to brown or this will make the sauce bitter.

Add the cream, salt, and pepper. Continue to simmer the sauce to allow the cream to reduce by 25 percent, about 20 minutes. Stir often during this process. Remove from heat and stir to recombine the butter and cream. Note: This step helps prevent the butter from separating.

Transfer to a shallow container and refrigerate until needed.

CLASSIC CLAM LINGUINE

Serves 2

Here's a classic Italian restaurant dish, and one of the simplest pasta dishes you can make at home. The recipe calls for Manila (or other small) clams, which are readily available at most supermarkets. They are usually sold on ice or in mesh bags because they are alive and need to breathe. If your fishmonger places them in a plastic bag, remove them from the bag when you get home and place them in a bowl (uncovered) in the refrigerator until ready to use. The other key to this dish is cooking your linguine less than what the package instructs. You want the pasta very al dente because it will continue to cook once it's added to the pan along with the clams.

Place the canned clams with their juice into a blender. Pulse several times, leaving it slightly chunky. Set aside.

Prepare the linguine by boiling it in a pot of unsalted water (no need for salt, there is plenty in the clam juice and Shellfish Herb Mix). Cook the pasta according to package directions but stop short as you want the pasta very al dente (the pasta will finish cooking later). Strain the pasta and set aside.

In a large sauté pan over medium heat, add the olive oil, Shellfish Herb Mix, and clams. Sauté to soften the garlic in the Mix, but do not brown. Add the blended clams, wine, and reserved linguine. Toss quickly and cover the pan to steam open the clams.

Once the clams begin to open, remove the lid, and reduce the liquid until it's saucy (not a broth). This is very important. Then remove and discard any unopened clams.

Transfer the pasta to an entrée plate, and mound in the center. Pour the remaining sauce over the top, garnish with parsley, and serve immediately.

1 (6.5 ounce) can of clams with juice

3¾ ounce dry linguine

3 tablespoons olive oil

2 to 3 tablespoons Shellfish Herb Mix, recipe follows

1 pound live Manila (or other small) clams

¾ cup white wine

1 teaspoon chopped fresh Italian flat leaf parsley, for garnish

SHELLFISH HERB MIX

1 tablespoon olive oil

2 tablespoons peeled and finely diced garlic

¼ to ½ teaspoon crushed red pepper (depending on your desired heat level)

⅛ teaspoon fresh cracked black pepper

½ teaspoon undiluted clam base ("Better Than Bouillon Clam Base," available online)

In a mixing bowl, add the olive oil, garlic, crushed red pepper, black pepper, and clam base. Mix well to combine and store in the refrigerator (up to 4 days) until ready to use or freeze for up to 3 months in a sealed container.

2 tablespoons olive oil

6 ounces bacon, cut into thin strips

2½ pounds skin-on, bone-in chicken thighs (about 6 total)

Kosher salt, as needed

2 medium onions, peeled and finely chopped (about 3 cups)

1 or 2 fennel bulbs, finely chopped (about 2 cups), plus ¼ cup coarsely chopped fronds for garnish

6 sprigs fresh thyme

½ cup dry white wine

¼ cup whole milk

¼ cup heavy cream

1 cup shelled fresh peas (from about 1 pound of pods) or frozen peas, thawed

Fresh cracked black pepper, as needed

11 ounces fresh (or dried) pappardelle

2 tablespoons butter, cut into pieces

½ cup finely grated fresh Parmigiano-Reggiano cheese, plus some shaved for garnish

2 tablespoons finely chopped fresh Italian flat leaf parsley

PAPPARDELLE WITH CHICKEN RAGÙ, FENNEL & PEAS

Most ragùs call for beef, pork, or veal, but sometimes I prefer chicken, particularly chicken thighs. Chicken thighs are an excellent choice for ragù because the dark meat benefits from "low and slow" methods like braising and stewing. When making this at home, browning the chicken is an important first step—not just for color, but for flavor. The chicken thighs seared in fat create new flavor compounds while simmering in just enough water to cover the chicken allows the muscle fibers and connective tissues to soften, resulting in tender, moist thigh meat.

In a large, wide saucepan or Dutch oven over medium heat, add the oil. When hot, add the bacon and cook, stirring often, until browned and crisp, about 5 minutes. Transfer the bacon with a slotted spoon to a small bowl.

Increase the heat to medium-high. Season the chicken thighs liberally with salt, then set them in the pan, skin-side down. Cook, turning halfway through, until golden brown on both sides, about 6 minutes total. Transfer to a plate.

Pour off all but 2 tablespoons of fat from the pan. Add the onions and fennel and cook, stirring occasionally, until soft and golden, 6 to 8 minutes. Add the thyme and cook until fragrant, about 30 seconds. Add the wine and simmer, stirring and scraping up brown bits, until reduced by half, about 5 minutes. Return the bacon and chicken to the pan. Note: The chicken should fit snugly in a single layer. Add water to barely cover the chicken. Bring to a simmer, then reduce the heat to medium-low and cover with the lid cracked. Cook until the chicken is tender, 60 to 90 minutes.

Continued . . .

Transfer the chicken to a plate and let cool. Then finely shred the chicken meat, discarding the bones and skin. Note: You should end up with about 3 cups of meat.

Add the milk and cream to the pan and set over medium-high heat. Cook, stirring occasionally to prevent sticking, until the sauce is nearly reduced by half and slightly thickened, about 8 to 12 minutes. Add the peas and chicken to the sauce and cook until the peas are just tender, about 4 minutes for fresh peas and 2 minutes for frozen. Season the sauce with salt and plenty of pepper. Keep warm while you cook the pasta.

Cook the pasta in a large pot of salted boiling water, stirring occasionally, until very al dente. Drain, reserving 1 cup of the pasta water.

Add the pasta, butter, ½ cup grated Parmigiano-Reggiano, and ½ cup of the pasta water to the sauce and mix to coat the pasta with the sauce. Increase heat to medium and continue cooking, stirring, and adding more cooking liquid as needed if sauce is too thick, until the butter and cheese are melted and incorporated into the sauce and the pasta is well coated. Add the parsley and toss to incorporate. Remove the woody stems from the thyme.

Divide the pasta among individual serving bowls and garnish with the fennel fronds and shaved Parmigiano-Reggiano cheese.

Pappardelle is a type of pasta that's cut into long, flat noodles. You can find it as fresh or dried egg pasta, and durum wheat pasta without eggs.

The nice, wide size of pappardelle makes it ideal in pasta dishes with rich, hearty sauces like ragùs.

3 tablespoons olive oil, divided

4 cloves garlic, lightly smashed and peeled

4 anchovy fillets

1 (24-ounce) jar Classico Pasta Sauce Traditional Sweet Basil

Fresh cracked black pepper, to taste

½ cup pitted kalamata olives

2 tablespoons capers, drained and rinsed

Crushed red pepper flakes, to taste

1 pound linguine, or other long pasta

2 tablespoons chopped fresh Italian flat leaf parsley, for garnish

½ teaspoon dry oregano, marjoram, or basil leaves, for garnish

Plenty of grated fresh Parmigiano-Reggiano cheese for serving

PASTA PUTTANESCA

Pasta Puttanesca is an Italian dish invented in Naples in the mid-20th century and made typically with simple pantry staples like tomatoes, olive oil, olives, anchovies, chili peppers, capers, and garlic, along with a long noodle pasta. The word "puttanesca" literally translates to "in the style of the prostitute," pointing to one of the theories of how this tangy sauce was invented by prostitutes to entice potential clients in with its bold aroma. This recipe uses store-bought pasta sauce to ease the preparation, which still results in an excellent dish.

In a saucepan over medium-low heat, add two tablespoons of the olive oil. When warm, add the garlic and anchovies. Cook, stirring occasionally, until the garlic is lightly golden, about 2 minutes. Next, add the jarred tomato sauce, along with some cracked black pepper. Increase the heat to medium-high and cook, stirring occasionally, about 10 minutes. Stir in the olives, capers, and red pepper flakes, and continue to simmer.

Cook the pasta, stirring occasionally, until the noodles are tender but not mushy. Drain quickly and toss with the sauce and remaining tablespoon of olive oil. Taste and adjust the seasonings as necessary. Garnish with the herbs and cheese and serve immediately.

¾ cup Meat Sauce, recipe follows

½ cup Garlic Cream Sauce, recipe follows

8 ounces cooked tagliatelle pasta, drained

1 tablespoon grated fresh Parmigiano-Reggiano cheese

Chopped fresh Italian flat leaf parsley, for garnish

MEAT SAUCE

¼ teaspoon kosher salt

1 pound 80/20 ground beef

1 pound ground hot Italian sausage

2 tablespoons minced garlic

1 teaspoon red pepper flakes

1 large can (100-ounce) Italian peeled tomatoes

Continued . . .

TAGLIATELLE BOLOGNESE

Tagliatelle Bolognese is a staple of Italian cuisine. The first official Bolognese recipe appeared in Pellegrino Artusi's cookbook L'Arte di Mangiare Bene ("The Art of Eating Well") in 1891. Though the recipe has evolved since Artusi's original method, pasta enthusiasts will note one constant: for true authenticity, the meat-based ragù sauce must be served with tagliatelle because the long, wide noodle shape provides the ideal vehicle for the heavy sauce. At our Palomino restaurants, which were famous for their rustic European menus, we perfected our tagliatelle ragù with minced beef and sausage, tomatoes, and plenty of roasted bell peppers.

In a medium sauté pan over medium heat, add the Meat Sauce. Stir until hot. Then stir in the Cream Sauce until well incorporated. Let the sauce bubble then thicken, about 2 to 3 minutes. Add the pasta, coating the noodles with the sauce. Remove from the heat and top with fresh Parmigiano-Reggiano cheese and parsley. Serve immediately.

MEAT SAUCE

In a Dutch oven or heavy-bottomed stockpot over medium-high heat, sprinkle the salt on the bottom of the pot. This will help brown the meat and prevent sticking. Add the ground beef (about ¼ pound at a time), while breaking up the meat with a wooden spoon and browning the beef. Then add the sausage and continue with the same procedure. When both the beef and sausage are browned (do not overcook; keep medium rare), remove from the heat and drain the meat, discarding the fat. Return the meat to the pot and add the garlic,

Continued . . .

1 tablespoon minced fresh Italian flat leaf parsley

1 (12-ounce) jar roasted red bell peppers, chopped

1 tablespoon dried oregano

1 tablespoon kosher salt

1 teaspoon fresh cracked black pepper

¼ cup olive oil

Makes about 1½ cups

1 tablespoon butter

1 tablespoon minced garlic

1 cup heavy cream

1 tablespoon grated fresh Parmigiano-Reggiano cheese

Kosher salt and fresh cracked black pepper, to taste

red pepper flakes, tomatoes, parsley, roasted red bell peppers, oregano, salt, and pepper. Stir well until incorporated and simmer uncovered for about 30 minutes until the flavors blend and the sauce thickens. Remove from the heat and stir in the olive oil. Cool, transfer to a clean container(s), and refrigerate until ready to use.

GARLIC CREAM SAUCE

In a sauté pan over medium heat, melt the butter. Add the garlic and sauté, stirring frequently, until softened, about 2 to 3 minutes. Note: Do not brown the garlic. Add the heavy cream and stir until incorporated. Reduce the cream until it lightly coats the back of a spoon, about 4 to 5 minutes. Remove from heat, stir in the Parmigiano-Reggiano cheese, and season with salt and pepper. Keep warm until ready to use.

3 tablespoons soy sauce

2 tablespoons oyster sauce

2 tablespoons hoisin sauce

1 tablespoon toasted
sesame oil

¼ teaspoon five-spice
powder

1 pound boneless country-
style pork ribs, trimmed
of fat and sliced crosswise
into ⅛-inch pieces (use
pork tenderloin if ribs are
unavailable)

¼ teaspoon liquid
smoke, optional

½ cup low-sodium
chicken broth

1 teaspoon cornstarch

2 garlic cloves, peeled and
minced (about 2 teaspoons)

2 teaspoons grated fresh ginger

1½ tablespoons vegetable
oil, divided

¼ cup Chinese rice cooking
wine or dry sherry, divided

½ pound shiitake
mushrooms, stems trimmed,
caps cut in halves or thirds
(about 3 cups)

2 bunches scallions, whites
thinly sliced and greens cut
into 1-inch pieces (about
2 cups)

Continued . . .

PORK LO MEIN

Glance into a busy Chinese restaurant kitchen and you'll see cooks working with intense flames from the wok burners. Not only are the flames dazzling, but they help flavor stir-fry dishes with what is known as wok hei ("the breath of the wok"). The typical smoky flavor of restaurant style pork lo mein is imparted into the oil and noodles when they are slightly singed by the fire. The liquid smoke included in this recipe's pork marinade repli-cates this traditional flavor. Be sure to prepare the ingredients ahead of time so this dish will flow quickly.

Bring 4 quarts water to boil in a Dutch oven over high heat.

In a medium bowl, add the soy sauce, oyster sauce, hoisin sauce, sesame oil, and five-spice powder. Mix well to combine. Place 3 tablespoons of the soy sauce mixture in a large ziplock bag. Add the pork and liquid smoke, if using. Press out as much air as possible and seal bag, making sure all the pieces are coated with the marinade. Refrigerate at least 15 minutes or up to 1 hour.

Add the broth and cornstarch into the remaining soy sauce mixture.

In a separate small bowl, mix the garlic and ginger with ½ tea-spoon of vegetable oil and set aside.

Heat 1 teaspoon of vegetable oil in a 12-inch cast-iron or nonstick skillet over high heat until just smoking. Add half of pork in a sin-gle layer, breaking up the clumps with a wooden spoon. Cook, without stirring, for 1 minute. Continue to cook, stirring occa-sionally, until browned, 2 to 3 minutes. Add 2 tablespoons of the wine to the skillet. Cook, stirring constantly, until the liquid is reduced, and the pork is well coated, 30 to 60 seconds. Transfer the pork to a medium bowl and repeat with the remaining pork, 1 teaspoon oil, and remaining 2 tablespoons wine.

Continued . . .

1 small head napa or Chinese cabbage (1½ pounds), halved, cored, and sliced crosswise into ½-inch strips (about 4 cups)

12 ounces fresh Chinese egg noodles or 8 ounces dried linguine or egg noodles

1 tablespoon Asian chili-garlic sauce

Wipe the skillet clean with paper towels. Return the skillet to high heat, add 1 teaspoon vegetable oil, and heat until just smoking. Add the mushrooms and cook, stirring occasionally, until light golden brown, 4 to 6 minutes. Add the scallions and continue to cook, stirring occasionally, until the scallions are wilted, 2 to 3 minutes longer. Transfer the vegetables to the bowl with the pork.

Add the remaining teaspoon of vegetable oil and cabbage to the now-empty skillet. Cook, stirring occasionally, until spotty brown, 3 to 5 minutes. Clear the center of the skillet and add the garlic-ginger mixture and cook, mashing mixture with spoon, until fragrant, about 30 seconds. Stir the garlic mixture into the cabbage. Return the pork-vegetable mixture and chicken broth–soy mixture to the skillet. Simmer until thickened and ingredients are well incorporated, 1 to 2 minutes. Remove skillet from the heat.

While the cabbage is cooking, cook the noodles in the boiling water. Stir occasionally, until the noodles are tender, 3 to 4 minutes for fresh noodles, about 10 minutes for dried noodles. Drain the noodles and transfer back to the Dutch oven. Add the cooked stir-fry mixture and chili-garlic sauce. Toss the noodles until well coated. Serve immediately.

What makes boneless country-style pork ribs most appealing is they are meatier than baby back or other ribs, and have some fat marbling, which makes cooking them more manageable than standard bone-in ribs.

FIVE-STAR

Beef Stroganoff 78

Brisket in Sweet-and-Sour Sauce 80

Chateaubriand with Chateaubriand Sauce 84

Chile-Braised Short Ribs 88

Classic Pot Roast with Carrot, Celery & Potato 90

Corned Beef Brisket with Apricot Glaze 92

Creamy Mushroom Meatloaf 94

Glazed Meatloaf 96

Old-Fashioned Beef Stew......................................98

Peppercorn-Crusted Roast Beef with

    Horseradish Cream 100

Slow Cooker Goulash with Parsley Pasta 104

Slow-Roasted Prime Rib 108

Steak Diane 112

BEEF, BEEF & MORE BEEF

BEEF STROGANOFF

1 pound 80/20 ground beef

Salt and fresh cracked black pepper, to season beef

3 tablespoons butter

8 ounces cremini mushrooms, thinly sliced (about 1½ cups)

¾ medium yellow onion, peeled and diced (about 1½ cups)

2 tablespoons dry sherry

1 beef bouillon cube, crushed

1 can (10.5 ounce) cream of mushroom soup

⅓ cup whole milk

⅔ cup heavy cream

½ teaspoon garlic powder

½ tablespoon ketchup

1 tablespoon minced fresh Italian flat leaf parsley (or ½ tablespoon dried)

½ tablespoon dry mustard

⅛ teaspoon fresh cracked black pepper, plus more to taste

¾ cup sour cream

Kosher salt, as needed, to taste

8 ounces cooked egg noodles, optional (or serve with rice)

During cold winter months, there's nothing more comforting than a dish of beef in a rich and creamy mushroom sauce. This recipe replaces chunks of beef with ground beef, which makes the dish easier to prepare and still just as good. Beef stroganoff, if you're curious, was created in Russia in the early 1800s by the personal chef of Count Stroganoff, a dignitary in the court of Alexander III. Today, beef stroganoff continues to grace tables across the globe.

In a large skillet or frying pan over medium-high heat, add the beef and season with salt and pepper. Brown the beef until no longer pink. Use a dough cutter to evenly break up the beef into small pieces. When the beef is cooked, drain the meat thoroughly and transfer to a bowl. Set aside.

Return the pan to the stove and reduce the heat to medium. Add the butter. When melted, add the sliced mushrooms. Sauté until soft and brown, 3 to 4 minutes. Remove the mushrooms from the pan and add the onions. Sauté until soft and golden brown, 3 to 5 minutes. Now, deglaze the pan with sherry. Return the cooked beef and mushrooms to the pan with the onions. Stir to combine, then stir in the beef bouillon, cream of mushroom soup, milk, cream, garlic powder, ketchup, parsley, dry mustard, and pepper. Reduce the heat to low and allow to simmer for 15 to 20 minutes, or until the mixture has thickened to your desired consistency. Remove from heat and allow to sit for several minutes before folding in the sour cream until well blended. Season with salt and pepper and serve immediately over hot, cooked egg noodles or rice.

BRISKET IN SWEET-AND-SOUR SAUCE

1 (3 to 6 pound) brisket, trimmed of almost all the fat, rinsed, and patted dry

1 medium yellow onion, peeled and rough chopped

1 (2-inch) piece fresh ginger, peeled and cut into chunks

6 large garlic cloves, peeled

1 cup ketchup

½ cup dry red wine

¼ cup cider vinegar

¼ cup soy sauce

¼ cup honey

¼ cup Dijon mustard

1 tablespoon coarsely ground fresh black pepper, or to taste

¼ teaspoon ground cloves

1½ cups Original Taste Coca-Cola

½ cup olive oil

Brisket is a workhorse cut of beef and this recipe can provide many servings for a good size gathering. Coca-Cola does its job of both tenderizing and adding a layer of caramel flavoring to the marinade/sauce. Ginger, mustard, wine, and vinegar add to its flavor. If you aren't familiar, a whole beef brisket consists of two parts: the flat cut and the point cut. I like the point cut as it is a thicker, more tender, moister meat that contains more fat. You can make this straightforward recipe in one day, but if you plan ahead and prepare it a day or two before, the two-step process is well worth the time. The slow-cooked, sliced brisket melts in your mouth, and the taste is amazing.

Allow the brisket to stand at room temperature for at least 30 minutes before cooking.

Preheat the oven to 325°F.

In a food processor or kitchen blender, add the onion, ginger, garlic, ketchup, wine, vinegar, soy sauce, honey, mustard, pepper, and cloves. Blend until the mixture is smooth. Transfer to a large mixing bowl, and slowly whisk in the cola and olive oil until incorporated.

Place the brisket, fat-side up, in a roasting pan just large enough to hold it. Pour the mixture over the top. Cover tightly with a lid or aluminum foil and transfer to the preheated oven. Bake for 2½ hours. Remove from the oven and carefully turn over the brisket. Ladle sauce over the top of the brisket, and cover. Return the pan to the oven and bake for an additional 2 to 2½ hours, or until the brisket is fork-tender. Note: A 3-pound brisket will cook much faster than a 6-pound piece. Remove from the oven and allow to cool completely. Then transfer to the refrigerator and cool overnight.

Continued . . .

The next day, preheat the oven to 300°F.

Transfer the brisket to a cutting board and thinly slice across the grain and set aside.

Remove any congealed fat from the top of the sauce, and discard. Transfer the skimmed sauce to an ovenproof pot over medium-high heat and bring to a boil. Note: If you feel the sauce should be reduced, boil for several minutes longer, or as needed. Remove the sauce from the heat and add the sliced brisket to the sauce. Stir to incorporate and transfer to the preheated oven. Warm for 15 minutes then serve immediately.

One of the key ingredients in Coca-Cola is phosphoric acid. The acid is what gives the bubbly beverage its tang. When added to a piece of meat, like brisket, the phosphoric acid breaks down proteins and connective tissue, making the cola an ideal ingredient in marinades.

1 (32-ounce) center-cut prime beef tenderloin

2 teaspoons Lawry's Seasoned Salt

Chateaubriand Sauce, recipe follows

CHATEAUBRIAND WITH CHATEAUBRIAND SAUCE

If you're looking for the perfect roast to celebrate a special occasion or holiday, look no further than the chateaubriand. Originating in France, the chateaubriand is the beautiful center cut of beef tenderloin that's meant for serving at least two people. It's also one of the most expensive cuts of beef and for good reason. The cut provides the most naturally tender piece of beef available. This elegant dish is easy to prepare. The beef is seasoned and grilled then sliced and served with a traditional shallot and wine sauce.

Preheat an outdoor or gas grill to medium-high heat.

Lightly season the beef tenderloin with the seasoned salt. Place on the barbecue and grill all sides until desired degree of doneness, about 20 minutes for medium rare (internal temperature should read 115 to 125°F), depending on the thickness of the cut. Remove from the heat and let rest for 10 minutes. Transfer the beef tenderloin to a cutting board atop a serving platter. Slice tableside and serve with the Chateaubriand Sauce.

Chateaubriand Sauce recipe on page 86

4 cups beef stock

1 cup red wine, preferably pinot noir

2 tablespoons finely chopped shallots

1 tablespoon finely chopped garlic

½ cup butter

8 ounces cremini mushrooms sliced into ¼-inch pieces (about 1 cup)

4 ounces shiitake mushrooms, stems removed, sliced into ¼-inch pieces (about ½ cup)

2 tablespoons cognac

2 tablespoons all-purpose flour

1 teaspoon finely chopped fresh rosemary

1 teaspoon finely chopped fresh thyme leaves

½ teaspoon kosher salt

½ teaspoon fresh cracked black pepper

½ teaspoon lemon zest

½ teaspoon granulated sugar

1 teaspoon Dijon mustard

¼ cup finely chopped fresh Italian flat leaf parsley

½ cup butter, cold and cut into cubes

CHATEAUBRIAND SAUCE

In a small saucepan over medium-high heat, add the beef stock and reduce by half of total amount (2 cups out of 4), about 20 minutes. Add the red wine, shallots, and garlic and continue simmering until reduced by half of total amount (1½ cups), about another 20 minutes. Remove from the heat and set aside.

In a large saucepan over medium heat, melt the butter. When melted, add the mushrooms. Sauté until tender then deglaze the pan with the cognac. Add the flour and stir until combined. Next, stir in the rosemary, thyme, salt, pepper, lemon zest, sugar, and mustard. Allow the sauce to come to a boil then remove from heat and stir in the reserved beef stock and wine. Stir in the parsley and set aside until the beef is ready to be plated. At the last minute, return the sauce to the pan over medium heat to reheat. When warm, add the cold butter cubes, one cube at a time, while stirring. When the last cube has been added, remove the sauce from the heat and pour ½ cup over each serving (off center as to avoid covering the beef completely).

It is essential to let the chateaubriand rest, and there's a reason why. As meat cooks, the juices and moisture inside rise to the surface. If you slice the meat as soon as it's finished cooking, the juices will spill out and pool onto your cutting board, resulting in a dry piece of meat. By letting the meat rest, you allow the muscle fibers time to relax while the juices get redistributed throughout, resulting in a juicier cut.

CHILE-BRAISED SHORT RIBS

Ingredients

2½ pounds cross-cut, bone-in short ribs (flanken style, 2 inches thick), cut into 2-inch cubes

Kosher salt, as needed

2 dried guajillo or ancho chiles, seeds removed

1 large yellow onion, peeled and sliced into ½-inch rounds

5 garlic cloves, unpeeled

1 teaspoon red pepper flakes

1 teaspoon ground coriander

1 teaspoon ground cumin

½ teaspoon ground cinnamon

3 tablespoons vegetable oil, divided

2 tablespoons tomato paste

½ acorn squash (about 1 pound), seeds removed, sliced lengthwise into 1-inch wedges

Plain whole-milk Greek yogurt, as needed, for garnish

Fresh cilantro sprigs, as needed, for garnish

Lime wedges, as needed, for garnish

This recipe with tender, fall-off-the-bone beef short ribs is the ideal meal on a cozy Sunday afternoon. For the short ribs, I use a flanken-style cut. That means the rib is cut across the bone so that each slice contains a few pieces of bone—and I like the bone for added flavor when simmering the meat. If you can't find short ribs precut flanken-style, ask your butcher to cut them for you.

Season the ribs with salt. Let sit at room temperature for 1 hour, or chill, uncovered, for up to 12 hours. Note: If chilling, bring the meat to room temperature (about 1 hour) before cooking. Next, place the chiles and 5 cups hot water in a kitchen blender and set aside. Broil the onion and garlic on a rimmed baking sheet, undisturbed, until charred and blistered on top, about 8 to 10 minutes. Remove the garlic cloves from their skins and place the garlic and charred onion, along with the red pepper flakes, coriander, cumin, and cinnamon, in the blender with the chiles. Blend until smooth. Season the puree lightly with salt. Set aside.

In a heavy medium-sized pot over medium-high heat, add 2 tablespoons of the vegetable oil. When hot, add half of the seasoned ribs, turning occasionally and reducing heat if needed, until browned on all sides, about 10 to 12 minutes per batch. Transfer the ribs to a plate and continue with the remaining ribs. When finished, carefully remove the hot oil and wipe out the pot. Add the remaining tablespoon of oil and place the pot back over medium-high heat. Add the tomato paste and cook, stirring often, about 3 minutes. Stir in the chile puree. Return the ribs to the pot and bring the liquid to a simmer. Partially cover the pot and cook, reducing the heat to low and turning ribs occasionally, while skimming any excess fat from the surface, until the meat is tender, about 3 hours. Note: If the sauce gets too thick, add some water. Next, add the squash. Bring to a simmer and cook, uncovered, until the squash is tender, and the liquid is thickened, about 30 minutes. Serve the ribs and squash, topped with yogurt and cilantro, with lime wedges.

4 pound beef chuck roast

Salt, as needed, for seasoning

Garlic powder, as needed, for seasoning

Fresh cracked black pepper, as needed, for seasoning

2 tablespoons olive oil

2 medium yellow onions, peeled, halved, and then each half quartered (8 pieces), divided

2 tablespoons tomato paste

4 cloves garlic, peeled and smashed

1 cup red wine plus more, if needed

1 cup chicken stock plus more, if needed

½ cup water plus more, if needed

1½ tablespoons Worcestershire sauce

1 cube beef bouillon, crumbled

1 can cream of mushroom soup

2 bay leaves

1 tablespoon fresh Italian flat leaf parsley, chopped

1 tablespoon peppercorns

3 sprigs fresh thyme sprigs

3 carrots, peeled and cut into 1-inch cubes

3 ribs celery, cut into 1-inch cubes

1 potato, cut into 1-inch cubes

CLASSIC POT ROAST WITH CARROT, CELERY & POTATO

One of the rules in my kitchen is to never rush a pot roast. You'll be disappointed if you try. Perfecting this dish requires one key ingredient—patience. Add that and the rest will fall into place. This chuck roast, surrounded by plenty of herbs, fresh vegetables, and a hearty liquid boasting of excellent flavor and texture, is easy and very good.

Cut the roast into four pieces. This will provide more surface to brown. Season the pieces liberally with salt, garlic powder, and pepper. Massage the seasoning into the meat, then bring the roast to room temperature, about 1 hour.

Preheat the oven to 285°F.

In a large skillet over high heat, add the olive oil. When hot, add the roast pieces and sear on all sides until well browned. Remove from the skillet and place the roast in a Dutch oven.

Return the skillet to the high heat and add the sectioned onion. Stirring frequently, brown the onion, but do not burn, about 3 minutes. Stir in the tomato paste and garlic. Continue to stir until the paste is evenly distributed and changing color. Stir in 1 cup of the wine, 1 cup of the chicken stock, and ½ cup of the water. Deglaze the pan while the liquid reduces by ¼, about 3 minutes. Stir in the Worcestershire sauce, crumbled beef bouillon cube, and cream of mushroom soup. Bring to a boil, then remove from heat and pour over the roast pieces in the Dutch oven. Add the bay leaves, parsley, peppercorns, and thyme sprigs to a sachet and place in the Dutch oven. Note: The liquid/sauce should cover the meat by about ¾. If not, add a little more wine, chicken stock, and water to raise to the appropriate level.

Place the Dutch oven in the preheated oven and cook for 2 hours. After 2 hours, add the carrots and celery and return to the oven to cook for 1 hour. After 1 hour, add the cubed potatoes and return to the oven to cook for 1 hour (4 hours total). The roast pieces should be tender and falling apart. If not, continue to roast until ready. Remove from the oven, discard the herb sachet, and serve the meat with the vegetables and sauce from the Dutch oven.

CORNED BEEF BRISKET WITH APRICOT GLAZE

1 (3½) pound uncured and brined corned Angus beef brisket

Original Taste Coca-Cola, as needed

Apricot Glaze, as needed, recipe follows

APRICOT GLAZE

½ cup apricot preserves

¼ cup brown sugar

1 tablespoon Dijon mustard

Corned beef is an Irish American favorite and the go-to meal for Saint Patrick's Day celebrations across the United States. But you may be surprised to learn corned beef is an American, not Irish, signature dish. In our home, I enjoy a good corned beef and it doesn't get any simpler than this recipe, made with another American classic—Coca-Cola. The Coke, thanks to the sugar and acid, makes a good meat tenderizer while adding flavor.

Preheat the oven to 320°F.

Pat the brisket dry with paper towels and place in a roasting pan. Fill the pan halfway up to the thickness of the corned beef with Coca-Cola. Bake covered in the oven until fork-tender, about 4½ hours. Remove from the oven and remove the meat from the pan. Place on a rimmed baking sheet and slather the corned beef with the Apricot Glaze. Heat the oven to broil and return the corned beef to the oven. Broil until the glaze is bubbling and caramelized, and a few black spots appear, about 1 or 2 minutes. Note: Charred, crisp spots dotting the surface is okay. Remove from the oven and allow to rest for 15 minutes. Slice the corned beef on the diagonal and serve.

APRICOT GLAZE

In a small bowl, add the apricot preserves, brown sugar, and mustard. Mix well to combine and brush liberally over the brisket.

½ pound 80/20 ground beef

½ pound ground pork

½ pound ground veal

1 medium onion, peeled and finely chopped (about 1½ cups)

1 cup Italian-seasoned dried breadcrumbs

1 large egg, beaten

½ teaspoon salt

½ teaspoon fresh cracked black pepper

CREAMY MUSHROOM SAUCE

¼ cup (4 tablespoons) butter

2 cups shiitake mushroom caps, sliced

3 tablespoons all-purpose flour

2½ cups low-sodium chicken or beef broth

1 teaspoon chopped fresh rosemary

½ teaspoon salt

½ teaspoon fresh cracked black pepper

½ cup heavy cream

CREAMY MUSHROOM MEATLOAF

During the Great Depression, meatloaf's popularity increased tenfold and became commonplace at the dinner table. There seems to be endless recipes and even more ingredients for meatloaf than can be counted. Be that as it may, the end game is that meatloaf is not only a popular dinner dish, but when prepared with a little creativity, such as adding a creamy mushroom sauce, meatloaf makes for an excellent meal.

Preheat the oven to 325°F.

In a large bowl, add the beef, pork, veal, onion, breadcrumbs, egg, salt, and pepper. Mix with hands until well blended, but do not overmix. Transfer the mixture to a 2-quart baking dish (about 7 × 11 inches), then form into a loaf shape. Set aside.

In a skillet over medium-high heat, add the butter. When melted, add the mushrooms and cook until they begin to brown, about 5 minutes. Add the flour and cook while stirring for 2 minutes. Add the broth, rosemary, salt, and pepper. Stir to incorporate and bring to a boil. When boiling, reduce the heat to a low simmer until the sauce begins to thicken, 1 to 2 minutes. Remove from the heat and stir in the cream.

Spoon all the mushroom mixture over the meatloaf and transfer to the oven. Bake until the internal temperature of the meatloaf reaches 150°F, about 1 hour, 15 minutes. Remove the meatloaf from the oven and let cool slightly before transferring to a serving platter.

2 pieces bacon, chopped

1 tablespoon extra-virgin olive oil

1 small yellow onion, peeled and finely diced (about 1 cup)

Kosher salt, as needed

3 cloves garlic, peeled and minced

½ cup whole milk

1 tablespoon Dijon mustard

1 tablespoon Worcestershire sauce

1 teaspoon hot sauce

2 large eggs, beaten

Fresh cracked black pepper, as needed

1 pound 80/20 ground beef

½ pound ground pork

½ pound ground veal

1 cup crushed saltine crackers (about 24 crackers)

⅓ cup minced fresh Italian flat leaf parsley

1½ tablespoons grated fresh Parmigiano-Reggiano cheese

THE GLAZE

½ cup Sweet Baby Ray's Original Barbecue Sauce (or similar sauce)

½ cup lightly packed brown sugar

¼ cup apple cider vinegar

1 tablespoon sriracha

GLAZED MEATLOAF

The first recorded recipe for the modern American meatloaf dates back to the late 1870s. That's according to the food historian Andrew Smith, who instructed the cook to finely chop "whatever cold meat you have." That meat, he said, would likely be beef, as New Englanders used every bit of the meat from their cows. Meatloaf was the answer. To the chopped beef, they added pepper, salt, onion, slices of milk-soaked bread and egg. You'll find these ingredients and steps in many meatloaf recipes today.

Preheat the oven to 325°F.

In a medium skillet over medium heat, add the bacon. Cook until stiff, but not crisp. Remove the bacon and drain on a paper-lined plate while reserving the bacon fat. Next, add the olive oil to the pan. When hot, add the onion and sauté, stirring often, until soft and translucent, 3 to 5 minutes. Season with salt and add the garlic. Sauté, stirring often to not burn the garlic, until soft, about 2 minutes. Remove from heat and let cool.

In a large mixing bowl, add the milk, mustard, Worcestershire, hot sauce, and eggs, then season with salt and pepper. Add the beef, pork, and veal along with the crackers, parsley, reserved bacon and bacon fat, cheese, and cooked onion-garlic mixture. Mix by hand until all the ingredients are incorporated. Do not overmix or it can result in a dense, tough loaf.

Transfer the meatloaf mixture to a parchment-lined baking sheet and form the mixture into a loaf shape, about 5 × 9 inches.

To make the Glaze, add the barbecue sauce, sugar, vinegar, and sriracha in a bowl. Whisk well to combine, then brush the loaf on the top and sides with the glaze.

Place the loaf in the oven and bake until the internal temperature of the loaf reaches 170°F, about 1 hour, 15 minutes. Baste the loaf once more halfway through the baking process. Remove from the oven and let rest for 20 minutes before applying more glaze. Then slice and serve.

OLD-FASHIONED BEEF STEW

2 tablespoons vegetable oil

¼ cup all-purpose flour

¼ teaspoon fresh cracked black pepper

1 pound beef stew meat, trimmed and cut into 1-inch cubes (about 30 pieces)

2 tablespoons red wine vinegar

1 cup red wine

3½ cups beef stock

2 bay leaves

1 medium yellow onion, peeled and chopped (about 1½ cups)

3 to 4 medium carrots, peeled and sliced into ¼-inch rounds (about 3 cups)

2 large russet baking potatoes, peeled and cut into ¾-inch cubes (about 3 cups)

2 teaspoons salt

This recipe is versatile and easy to put together, resulting in a stew that's savory and comforting. Most grocery stores offer stew meat, already cut, which is usually just a cubed chuck roast— perfect for this dish. When cooked slowly over a long period of time, the roast ends up extremely tender.

Heat a Dutch oven or other heavy-bottomed pot over medium-high heat. Add the vegetable oil.

In a bowl, combine the flour and pepper, then add the cubed meat and toss to coat, shaking off excess.

When the oil is hot, add the beef in batches (about 10 pieces at a time) to not overcrowd the pot. When browned on all sides (about 5 minutes per batch; adding more oil as necessary), remove the meat from the pan and set aside. Next, deglaze the pot with the vinegar and wine, stirring to loosen any browned bits off the bottom. Return the beef to the pot, along with the beef stock and bay leaves. Bring to a boil then reduce to a simmer. Allow to simmer, stirring occasionally, until the beef is soft and tender, about 1½ hours. Add the onion and carrots and continue to simmer for 15 minutes. Add the potatoes and simmer for another 30 to 40 minutes, or until the potatoes are fork-tender. Season the stew with salt, to taste, and serve.

PEPPERCORN-CRUSTED ROAST BEEF WITH HORSERADISH CREAM

¼ cup coarsely cracked black peppercorns

2 tablespoons coarse kosher salt, plus more to taste (try Diamond Crystal)

2 tablespoons fresh rosemary leaves, plus 2 (5-inch) fresh rosemary sprigs, broken in half, divided

¼ cup Dijon mustard

1 (4 to 5 pound) boneless New York strip, excess fat pockets removed

1 large yellow onion, peeled and coarsely chopped (about 2½ cups)

3 ribs celery, coarsely chopped (about 1 cup)

1 medium carrot, coarsely chopped (about ½ cup)

5 garlic cloves

2½ tablespoons butter

2½ tablespoons all-purpose flour

2 cups chicken stock

Horseradish Cream, as needed, recipe follows

What a big surprise this dish turned out to be. I knew a roasted New York strip would be good, but wow, this is crazy good. Instead of the usual and delicious prime rib (page 108), I purchased a four-pound prime New York strip. I removed all the outside fat, thinned the fat pockets, and coated the beef in a mixture of mustard, peppercorns, salt, and fresh rosemary leaves. An overnight chill in the refrigerator seasoned the beef while drying the outside, resulting in a crispy crust after roasting. What I found so amazing is after the slow roast, the beef texture resembled prime rib more than New York steak, but with a more pronounced flavor and mouthfeel.

In a small bowl, add the cracked peppercorns, salt, and rosemary leaves. Mix well.

Rub the mustard all over the meat. Then sprinkle evenly with the peppercorn mixture, pressing to adhere. Place the meat on a wire rack set inside a rimmed baking sheet. Refrigerate, uncovered, at least 12 hours or up to 26 hours. When ready to cook, remove the meat from the refrigerator and bring to room temperature, about 1 hour.

Preheat oven to 450°F.

In a 12 × 16-inch roasting pan, add the onion, celery, carrot, garlic, and the 2 rosemary sprigs. Place the room-temperature seasoned beef on top of the vegetable mixture. Roast in the preheated oven on the middle rack for 15 minutes without opening

the oven. Reduce the oven temperature to 270°F. Continue roasting until a thermometer inserted into the thickest portion of the meat registers 115°F, about 1 hour to 1 hour, 30 minutes. Note: Check the internal temperature of the meat at 45 minutes. When the meat reaches temperature, remove the roasting pan from the oven. Transfer the beef to a cutting board and let rest for 20 minutes. (Internal temperature will continue to climb to 125°F.)

While the roast rests, place the roasting pan on the stovetop over medium heat. Add the butter to the vegetable mixture in the pan and cook, stirring constantly, until melted. Sprinkle the flour over the mixture and continue to cook, stirring constantly for 2 minutes. Gradually add the stock, whisking constantly, until mixture is smooth. Bring the mixture to a simmer over medium heat, and allow to simmer, whisking often, until thickened, about 3 to 4 minutes. Season the gravy with additional salt, to taste. Pour the gravy through a fine wire-mesh strainer into a small bowl, discarding the vegetables and solids, and transfer the gravy to a gravy boat.

Slice the beef into ½-inch-thick slices, and transfer to a large platter. Serve with the gravy and Horseradish Cream.

HORSERADISH CREAM

In a bowl, add the sour cream, horseradish, salt, and pepper. Whisk until well combined. Cover and refrigerate until ready to use.

2 cups sour cream

½ cup prepared horseradish, well drained

2 teaspoons coarse kosher salt

1 teaspoon fresh cracked black pepper

1 (3-pound) boneless beef chuck roast, cut into 3 or 4 pieces

Coarse kosher salt, as needed

Fresh cracked black pepper, as needed

¼ cup all-purpose flour

2 tablespoons olive oil

1 large onion, peeled and diced (about 2 cups)

1 large beet (or 2 medium), peeled and diced (about 2 cups)

3 large celery ribs, diced (about 1 cup)

1 large carrot (or 2 or 3 medium), peeled and sliced ¼ inch thick (about 1 cup)

¼ cup tomato paste

2 tablespoons minced garlic

2 tablespoons sweet Hungarian paprika

2 teaspoons ground cumin

2 teaspoons coriander

1 teaspoon caraway seeds

½ cup dry red wine

1½ cups beef broth

¼ cup chopped fresh Italian flat leaf parsley

2 teaspoons red wine vinegar

Parsley Pasta (page 106)

Sour cream, as needed, for garnish

SLOW COOKER GOULASH WITH PARSLEY PASTA

Traditional Hungarian goulash is a soup or stew that's usually filled with beef and onions spiced with paprika. It dates back centuries and was originally made by shepherds drying out meat to store and then adding water to create a soup or stew. This version features sweet Hungarian paprika and red beets. When making at home, it's important to coat the roast in flour before searing. The flour helps the meat develop a golden sear while adding body to the stew.

Bring the roast to room temperature, about 1 hour. Then coat the roast pieces liberally with salt, pepper, and flour, gently shaking off the excess.

In a large sauté pan over high heat, add the olive oil. When hot, add the meat and sear until deeply brown on all sides, about 12 minutes. Transfer the roast to a 6- or 7-quart slow cooker.

Reduce the pan heat to medium-high and add the onion, beets, celery, and carrots to the beef drippings, stirring occasionally, until softened, about 3 minutes. Add the tomato paste, garlic, paprika, cumin, coriander, and caraway seeds. Stir occasionally while cooking for another 2 minutes. Next, deglaze the pan with the red wine until nearly evaporated, about 1 minute. Add the broth, bring to a boil, then transfer the mixture to the slow cooker. Cover the slow cooker and cook the roast on low until fork-tender, about 6 to 6½ hours. Remove the meat and shred, discarding any fatty bits, then return the shredded meat to the cooker. Add the fresh parsley and red wine vinegar, stirring to incorporate. Season to taste with salt and pepper.

Serve the goulash over the Parsley Pasta and garnish with sour cream, if desired. Serve immediately.

Continued . . .

PARSLEY PASTA

1 pound pappardelle pasta

1 stick (8 tablespoons) butter

½ cup chopped fresh Italian flat leaf parsley

Salt and fresh cracked black pepper, to taste

Cook the noodles in a large pot of boiling salted water according to package directions. Drain the noodles and toss with the butter and fresh parsley. Season with salt and pepper and serve.

SLOW-ROASTED PRIME RIB

15 pounds USDA prime-grade prime rib, boneless

½ cup Lawry's Seasoned Salt

2 tablespoons fresh cracked black pepper

Note: For a 6-pound roast, use 3 ounces of the seasoned salt and 2 teaspoons pepper

In 1992, Roche Harbor Resort wanted to bring the prime rib served in New York steak houses to the Northwest marina. Since that time, we have perfected this recipe and are excited to share it with you. When preparing prime rib, there are three critical steps that must be followed: 1) select the best prime rib you can find. At Roche Harbor, we use USDA prime-grade prime rib that is aged for sixty days. 2) Cook the roast low and slow. And 3) after the prime rib is cooked to the correct temperature, keep it in a warm oven for at least 3 hours before serving. All three of these steps will guarantee a prime rib that is rich in beef flavor, tender to the bite, and cooked consistently through from end to end. This recipe calls for a 15-pound roast, but I've made it successfully with a roast as small as six pounds.

The equipment you will need for this recipe is: 1) a shallow roasting pan with a rack to elevate the prime rib above the pan. This will allow the prime rib to be exposed to even oven heat. 2) A digital probe-type meat thermometer with temperature alarm would be helpful. This will allow you to relax with confidence knowing the thermometer will read the internal temperature without you having to open the oven and check it every 15 minutes. Just set the alarm temperature to medium rare or 120°F and wait for the alarm. And 3) a standard oven thermometer that can be attached to the center oven rack. This should read the same temperature as the oven temperature. You may need to adjust your oven temperature to cook and hold the prime rib at the desired temperature.

Timing is everything when cooking prime rib. When planning a prime rib dinner, the question of when to start the prime rib is essential to a successful dinner. Start the prime rib six hours before dinner (at Roche Harbor the process can take up to

10 hours). For example, if dinner is planned at 6:00 p.m., the prime rib should enter the oven no later than 12:00 p.m. that afternoon. This allows for two or three hours of cooking time and two hours of warming time. While the cooking time is not exact, the warming time can last up to five hours. I know what you're thinking: "Holding a roast in the oven for more than two hours is going to continue to cook the meat and the prime rib will be well done by the time you serve dinner." Trust me. As long as the temperature in the oven that the prime rib is being held in does not exceed 140°F and does not drop below 120°F, the prime rib will rise in temperature only two or three degrees and the warming process will finish the meat to perfection. Later that evening, when you are slicing the prime rib, the meat will be firm and tender and will not bleed out on the plate.

At Roche Harbor, we cook our prime rib to medium rare, or 120°F to 125°F. Some guests may like their prime rib cooked a little more than medium rare, but remember, there will be two end cuts that will be more toward the medium side. If a medium prime rib is the goal, cook the prime to 125°F to 130°F.

Remove the prime rib from the refrigerator 2 hours before it needs to go into the oven. Place the prime rib on the rack of the shallow roasting pan. Rub the entire roast with the Lawry's Seasoned Salt and fresh cracked black pepper. Let the seasoned prime rib rest on the counter until ready to place in the oven. Allowing the roast to rest at room temperature will improve the flavor and tenderness of the prime rib.

Open the oven and adjust one of the oven racks to the center position. Place the standard oven thermometer on the center rack and set the oven temperature to 250°F. After the oven is preheated, check the dial on the standard thermometer; it should also read 250°F. If not, adjust the oven temperature so that the standard thermometer reads 250°F.

Place the prime rib on the roasting rack and pan and then in the center of the 250°F oven. Insert the probe of the digital thermometer into the center of one of the prime rib ends and push the probe deep into the roast. Plug the probe into the digital thermometer and adjust to 120°F and turn the alarm on. Monitor the temperature every half hour. When the prime rib internal temperature reaches 100°F, it will not be long before the prime rib reaches the ideal 120°F. Note: The temperature will rise rapidly.

When the prime rib hits 120°F, remove from the oven and let rest on the counter for 30 minutes. Open the oven door and allow the oven to cool down. Turn the oven temperature to 140°F. If the oven does not lower to 140°F, the oven will have to be turned off and then on again manually to maintain a temperature between 120°F and 140°F. Note: My oven has this challenge, and I have found that if I turn it to 175°F for five minutes and then turn it off, the 120°F to 140°F temperature range will last for 30 minutes.

Return the prime rib to the oven. Monitor the oven and internal prime rib temperature for the next 3 hours.

When ready to serve, place the prime rib, cut-side down, on a large cutting board. At this point, the tail fat must be trimmed before the roast is carved. There is usually a greater proportion of tail fat on the loin end following the contour of the rib. Trim the fat from the tail leaving no more than 1½ inches of tail fat. As a general rule, a 12-ounce restaurant cut will be 1 inch thick, or the distance between your thumbnail and first joint. Begin by slicing the first end cut and reserving it for a guest who prefers medium. Continue slicing and adjusting the thickness of the slice to the amount of prime rib each guest prefers.

Serve with fresh horseradish and au jus, if desired.

4 (8- to 10-ounce) center-cut beef tenderloin steaks, about 1¼ inch thick

½ cup beef broth

4 teaspoons Worcestershire sauce

2 teaspoons Dijon mustard

2 teaspoons tomato paste

2 tablespoons butter

½ cup finely minced shallots

4 tablespoons brandy or cognac

⅓ cup heavy cream

Fresh cracked black pepper, as needed

1 to 2 tablespoons finely chopped chives

STEAK DIANE

Steak Diane originated in the 1950s, and there are many versions of this dish. I find this simple recipe is one of the best. For searing, the best type of pan to use is a large cast-iron skillet. The cast iron distributes heat evenly, so the steaks sear quickly and cook evenly.

Place the beef tenderloin steaks on the kitchen counter to bring to room temperature (30 minutes to 1 hour).

In a small bowl, add the beef broth, Worcestershire sauce, mustard, and tomato paste. Whisk until combined. Set aside.

In a large skillet over medium-high heat, add the butter. Pat the steaks dry with paper towels and when the butter has completely melted, turn the heat to high. Add the steaks to the pan. Do not overcrowd the pan (you may need to cook in batches). Do not touch the steaks. For medium rare, sear for 5 to 6 minutes (depending on exact thickness of steak or desired doneness). Turn the steaks over and sear the other side for 5 to 6 minutes. Remove when the internal temperature of the steaks reaches 125°F (the temperature will continue to rise to 130°F, which is medium rare) and transfer to a plate. Cover with foil and let rest.

Reduce the heat to medium-high and add the shallots to the skillet. Stir occasionally so the shallots don't burn. Add the brandy or cognac to deglaze the pan. Caution: The alcohol will likely produce a flame as the liquor burns off. Continue to cook until the liquor has almost evaporated. Stir in the broth mixture and bring to a boil. Cook until the sauce has thickened, about 2 to 3 minutes. Stir in the cream and cook for 2 more minutes.

To serve, either slice the cooked steak on the bias into several ½-inch slices, then spoon the sauce on one side of the plate and lay the slices overlapping over the sauce, or place the entire, uncut steak onto the sauce. Garnish with fresh pepper and chives before serving.

FIVE-STAR

Braised Chicken Thighs with Potatoes, Porcini

& Cherries...116

Braised Chicken with Mustard....................................118

Chef John's Salt Roasted Chicken 122

Chicken Dijon 124

Chicken Francese 126

Chicken Piccata with Lemon, Butter

& Caper Sauce 130

Chicken Tikka Masala...134

Craig Claiborne's Smothered Chicken......................136

Fried Chicken with Chile Jam...................................140

Kung Pao Chicken 144

L&L Drive-Inn Lin-Katsu Chicken..............................146

Old-Fashioned Chicken Potpie.................................149

Pan-Seared Chicken with Riesling Cream Sauce

& Chanterelles...150

Pietro's Chicken Parmesan.......................................154

Roast Koji Chicken...158

CHICKEN MANY WAYS

BRAISED CHICKEN THIGHS WITH POTATOES, PORCINI & CHERRIES

1 teaspoon plus 1 tablespoon canola oil, divided

14 large garlic cloves, peeled (10 whole and 4 crushed)

1½ cups crème fraîche or sour cream

⅔ cup dried porcini mushrooms (about ½ ounce)

Kosher salt, as needed, to season

2 pounds large chicken thighs, skin on (5 to 8 thighs)

2 medium Yukon Gold potatoes, peeled and sliced ⅛ inch thick (about 3 to 3½ cups)

¼ to ½ cup unsweetened dried sour cherries (1 or 2 ounces)

Celery leaves, for optional garnish

Here's a delicious dish that combines chicken, potatoes, and porcini mushrooms with garlicky crème fraîche and dried cherries. Originally popularized in Italy, porcinis grow all around the world. That means you can find them dried in most markets and grocery stores. If you don't have crème fraîche, sour cream will work.

In a medium saucepan over low heat, add the teaspoon of oil. When the oil is warm, add the 10 whole garlic cloves and cook, stirring often, until golden and fragrant, about 5 minutes. Add 4½ cups water and bring to a boil. Cover the pan and simmer until the liquid is reduced by half; or about 2½ cups, about 1 hour. Strain the garlic broth into a bowl.

In another bowl, add 1½ cups of the garlic broth and whisk while adding the crème fraîche and dried mushrooms. Season with salt. Note: Reserve the extra garlic broth for another use.

Preheat the oven to 350°F.

In a large cast-iron skillet over medium heat, add the remaining tablespoon of oil. Season the chicken thighs with salt and add to the skillet. Note: Cook in 2 or more batches to not overcrowd the pan. Cook until the thighs are golden brown on both sides, about 5 minutes per side. Remove the chicken and transfer to a plate. Discard all but 1 tablespoon of the oil from the skillet. Arrange the potato slices in the pan, overlapping them slightly. Set the chicken thighs, skin-side down, on top of the potatoes. Scatter the cherries and crushed garlic cloves around the chicken and potatoes and top with the garlic sauce and porcinis.

Transfer to the preheated oven and roast for 20 minutes. Reduce the oven temperature to 300°F and roast for another 45 minutes, or until the potatoes are fork-tender and the chicken is cooked through.

Preheat the broiler and arrange the rack about 6 inches from the heat element. Turn the chicken skin-side up and broil until the skin is golden and crispy, about 5 minutes. Remove from the oven, garnish with celery leaves, if desired, and serve immediately.

BRAISED CHICKEN WITH MUSTARD

½ cup plus 3 tablespoons Dijon mustard

¼ teaspoon sweet or smoked paprika

Fresh cracked black pepper, as needed, to taste

¾ teaspoon kosher salt

4 chicken thighs plus 4 legs

4 slices smoked thick-cut bacon, diced

1 small onion, finely diced (about 1½ cups)

1 teaspoon fresh thyme leaves

Olive oil, as needed, for frying

1 cup white wine

1 tablespoon whole mustard seeds or whole grain mustard

4 tablespoons crème fraîche or heavy cream

Chopped fresh Italian flat leaf parsley or chives, as needed, for garnish

Chicken with Mustard is a classic French dish, also known as Poulet à la Moutarde. It's very simple and good. Chicken legs and thighs are pan-fried until crispy then braised in a white wine cream sauce spiked with Dijon. You might serve it alongside some mashed potatoes, a nest of fresh pasta, or a crusty baguette—the perfect vehicle for mopping up the sauce.

In a large bowl, add the ½ cup Dijon mustard, paprika, several grinds of the peppermill, and salt. Mix well to combine, then toss the chicken pieces into the mustard mixture, lifting the chicken skin and rubbing some of the mustard mixture beneath until well coated. Set aside.

In a Dutch oven or large skillet with a lid over medium-high heat, add the diced bacon. Cook, stirring frequently, until softened and just starting to brown, about 4 minutes. Do not crisp. Remove the bacon and drain on a plate lined with paper towels. Leave about 1½ tablespoons of bacon fat in the skillet, discarding the rest. Add the onion to the bacon drippings and cook for about 5 minutes, until soft and translucent. Stir in the thyme and let cook for several minutes, then scrape the cooked onion and thyme onto the bacon.

Add a little olive oil to the skillet, if necessary, and add the chicken pieces to the skillet in a single layer over medium-high heat. If the pieces don't all fit, cook in 2 batches as to avoid overcrowding the pan. Thorough browning is important, so brown the chicken well on one side, then turn over and brown the other side.

Remove the chicken pieces and transfer to the plate with the onions and bacon. Next, add the wine to the skillet, scraping the darkened bits off the bottom. Return the chicken pieces to the skillet along with the bacon and onions. Cover and cook

the chicken over low to medium heat, turning the pieces in the sauce a few times, until the chicken is cooked through, 15 to 25 minutes. Note: Use an instant-read thermometer to make sure the chicken's internal temperature doesn't exceed 160°F.

Remove the skillet from the heat. Arrange the chicken on a platter. Stir the remaining 3 tablespoons Dijon mustard, the mustard seeds or grainy mustard, and the crème fraîche or heavy cream into the pan drippings. If the sauce has reduced and is quite thick, you can thin it with a little warm water, adding a teaspoon or so at a time. Pour the sauce over the chicken, sprinkle chopped parsley over the top, and serve.

CHEF JOHN'S SALT-ROASTED CHICKEN

1 (4-pound) whole chicken, room temperature

3 tablespoons kosher salt, or more as needed

¾ tablespoon chopped fresh thyme leaves

1 tablespoon fresh lemon juice

½ cup chicken stock

3 tablespoons white wine

4 tablespoons cold butter, cut into pieces

Fresh cracked black pepper, to taste

1 pinch cayenne pepper, or to taste

If you're like me, I'm always on the lookout for new recipes to try. I also forget how good a homemade roast chicken can be. This dish is about encrusting the chicken (the smaller the chicken, the more tender and juicier) with kosher salt and cooking the bird so it crisps up in its own juices, resulting in moist and flavorful meat. Slice the chicken and serve with the thyme butter sauce made from the caramelized drippings.

Preheat the oven to 450°F.

Dry the chicken with paper towels. Season the entire chicken liberally, inside and out, with the salt. Be generous, as a salty crust is the key to this recipe. Using kitchen twine, tie the legs together and place in a large cast-iron skillet. Tuck the wings underneath the chicken so the tips don't burn or cut off the wing tips with a pair of kitchen scissors. Place the chicken in the preheated oven and roast until golden-brown and the chicken is cooked through, about 50 to 60 minutes. Remove from the heat and transfer the chicken to a serving platter and keep warm.

In the roasting skillet, remove about 90 percent of the chicken fat, keeping the crispy bits on the bottom of the pan. Place over medium heat and add the thyme leaves. Stir until wilted, about 2 minutes. Add the lemon juice, chicken stock, and wine. Deglaze the pan while stirring to scrape up the crispy bits (while discarding any large pieces of skin or fat that accumulated during the roasting process). Continue to stir until the liquid is reduced by half, about 2 minutes. Reduce the heat to low and stir in the butter, one piece at a time, along with any remaining juice from the chicken, until the sauce has thickened, about 1 minute. Remove from the heat and season with pepper and cayenne.

Carve the chicken, discarding the salt-skin crust, if desired, and spoon the sauce over the chicken. Serve immediately.

1¼ tablespoons minced fresh Italian flat leaf parsley, divided

2½ tablespoons fresh grated Parmigiano-Reggiano cheese, divided

½ cup Japanese-style panko breadcrumbs

2 tablespoons Dijon mustard, divided

2 tablespoons Best Foods or Hellmann's Real Mayonnaise

½ cup butter

1 teaspoon minced garlic

2 (8 ounce) boneless, skinless chicken breasts

CHICKEN DIJON

Another popular entrée from Restaurants Unlimited (served at Kincaid's Restaurants), nothing brings the taste buds alive like the combination of chicken and mustard. The star ingredient in this recipe is Dijon. Most true Dijons use black or brown mustard seeds, white wine, and a wide variety of other seasonings, giving the Dijon a pleasant, aromatic, and distinctive taste. Dijon enhances dressings, vinaigrettes, cheeses, and many types of meat dishes, particularly chicken, providing a tangy flavor that warms the soul. This recipe for Chicken Dijon uses Dijon in two steps: first as a moist coating before the cutlet is breaded and then as a topping when the baked cutlet is served.

In a mixing bowl, add 1 tablespoon of the parsley and 2 tablespoons of the cheese, along with the panko breadcrumbs. Mix until well combined. Set aside.

In a small bowl, add 1 tablespoon of Dijon mustard and the mayonnaise. Mix well to combine and set aside.

In a sauté pan over low heat, add the butter and garlic and sauté until fragrant, about 1 minute. Add the remaining tablespoon of mustard, remove from the heat, and whisk vigorously until the mixture thickens but doesn't separate.

Dip the chicken breasts into the butter-garlic mixture, coating all surfaces. Then dip into the parsley-cheese-breadcrumb mixture. Pack the crumbs onto the chicken and coat well. Transfer the breaded chicken breasts to the refrigerator to chill for at least 3 hours. This will help set the breading.

When ready to cook, preheat the oven to 375°F. Arrange the chicken breasts on a sheet pan and bake in the preheated oven until lightly brown and cooked through to an internal temperature of 140°F, about 25 minutes. Remove from the oven and transfer to a serving plate. Top with the remaining ¼ tablespoon parsley and ½ tablespoon cheese and serve with the Dijon-mayo sauce.

CHICKEN FRANCESE

2 eggs

2 tablespoons whole milk

½ teaspoon fresh cracked black pepper, plus more for seasoning

1 cup all-purpose flour

⅓ cup olive oil

⅓ cup vegetable oil

4 to 6 large boneless, skinless chicken breasts (2 to 2½ pounds), each breast sliced in half horizontally

6 tablespoons butter, divided

1 large lemon, thinly sliced (about 10 slices)

½ cup dry white wine

1 small lemon, juiced (about 3 tablespoons)

2 cups chicken stock

Salt, to taste

Cornstarch, as needed

2 tablespoons minced fresh Italian flat leaf parsley

Also called Chicken French, this restaurant-quality dish is easy to make at home with thin-sliced boneless, skinless chicken breasts cooked in a buttery, lemon pan sauce. To slice the breasts very thin, freeze the chicken breasts for about 15 minutes before slicing with a very sharp kitchen knife. Place each breast on a flat non-slip surface. Hold down the breast with your fingers or use a heavy weight. Slowly and carefully, slice the breast parallel with the surface until sliced through. You should end up with two thin slices about the same size.

In a bowl, add the eggs, milk, and pepper. Whisk until well combined. In a separate bowl, add the flour. Next, line a baking sheet with paper towels.

In a large skillet over medium heat, add the olive oil and vegetable oil until hot. Working in two batches, as to not overcrowd the pan, lightly dredge the chicken in the flour and shake off the excess. Then dip the chicken into the egg batter, letting excess batter drip back into the bowl, and carefully place in the skillet. Fry, turning once, until golden brown on both sides, about 3 to 4 minutes per side. Adjust the heat as the breasts cook (reducing to medium-low if necessary) so they brown slowly and evenly. It's best if the chicken is a little undercooked at this stage. They will finish cooking when added back to the pan.

Transfer the chicken to the paper-towel-lined baking sheet and repeat with the remaining breasts. When all the breasts are browned, remove the pan from the heat and discard the oil. Wipe the pan clean and return the pan to low heat. Add 3 tablespoons of the butter. When the butter is melted and sizzling, add the lemon slices. Cook, stirring occasionally, until the lemon slices are golden and browning around the edges, about 3 minutes per side. Remove the lemon slices and set aside.

Next, add the remaining 3 tablespoons of butter, along with the wine and lemon juice, and bring to a boil. Boil until the liquid is

syrupy, about 5 minutes. Add the chicken stock, bring to a boil, and cook until thickened, about 15 minutes. Taste and adjust the seasonings with lemon juice, salt, and pepper. The sauce should taste lemony, but not too lemony and not too salty. Reduce the heat, add the chicken back to the skillet and simmer gently until the sauce is velvety and the chicken is heated through, about 4 minutes. The sauce should continue to thicken when the chicken is added. If the sauce remains thin, add a little cornstarch slurry to thicken the sauce. Turn the chicken over and mop with the sauce. Place the cooked lemon slices on top. Sprinkle with chopped parsley and serve, spooning some of the sauce over each serving.

Chicken Francese often gets confused with chicken piccata. The difference is the order in which the chicken is dipped. Chicken Francese first dips the chicken in flour then the eggs while piccata dips the chicken in eggs followed by the flour. Capers are also typically added to the piccata.

CHICKEN PICCATA WITH LEMON, BUTTER & CAPER SAUCE

¾ cup finely grated fresh Parmigiano-Reggiano cheese

¼ cup all-purpose flour

2 eggs

4 boneless, skinless chicken breasts

½ cup olive oil

Lemon, Butter & Caper Sauce, as needed, recipe follows

When you and your family are craving a delicious weeknight dinner that's fast to make, try this lemony, caper-topped Italian American classic, from Longhi's Restaurant in Lahaina, Maui. Thin slices of boneless, skinless chicken breasts are crusted with Parmesan cheese and flour and then fried and smothered in a tangy lemon-butter pan sauce seasoned with white wine and capers. If you buy capers in brine, make sure to drain the liquid before adding them to this recipe. If your capers are packed in salt, give them a rinse, or soak them in water for several minutes before using.

Pound each chicken breast with a kitchen mallet between two pieces of plastic wrap to an even ⅓-inch thickness.

In a shallow bowl, combine the cheese and flour. Lightly beat the eggs in another bowl. Dip each chicken breast in the beaten eggs, then the cheese and flour mixture. Lay each breast on a plate and press more of the cheese mixture onto any exposed or thin areas.

In a large frying pan over medium heat, add the olive oil. When hot, add the chicken breasts. Fry in batches, likely two breasts at a time, as to not overcrowd and cool the pan. Fry until golden brown, about 3 minutes, then carefully turn over and fry the remaining side until golden brown and cooked through, about another 3 minutes. Remove from heat and transfer the breasts to individual serving plates. Pour the Lemon, Butter & Caper Sauce over each breast and serve.

1 cup white wine

3 ounces fresh lemon juice

5 tablespoons cold butter, cut into chunks

¼ cup capers, drained and rinsed

LEMON, BUTTER & CAPER SAUCE

In the large frying pan you used to fry the chicken breasts, drain off the excess juices and/or fat and place over medium heat. When hot, add the wine to the pan and reduce for 1 minute. Add the lemon juice and allow to simmer for several minutes, or until reduced by half. Stir in the cold butter, about 1 or 2 tablespoons at a time, adding more as the butter gets absorbed. Finish by adding the capers and stir until smooth and saucy, about another 8 minutes. Remove from the heat and pour over the chicken breasts just before serving.

CHICKEN TIKKA MASALA

2 tablespoons clarified butter (or ghee)

1 cup finely chopped onion

4 cloves garlic, peeled and minced

1 tablespoon ground cumin

1 teaspoon salt, or more to taste

1 teaspoon ground ginger

½ to 1 teaspoon cayenne pepper, depending on desired spice level

½ teaspoon ground cinnamon

¼ teaspoon ground turmeric

1 (15-ounce) can tomato sauce

1 cup heavy cream

1 tablespoon white sugar, or more to taste

2 teaspoons sweet paprika

1 tablespoon vegetable oil

4 skinless, boneless chicken breast halves (about 1½ pounds), cut into bite-size pieces

½ teaspoon curry powder

Chopped fresh cilantro, as needed, for garnish

Hot cooked rice or naan bread, as needed for serving, optional

Indian food aficionados are familiar with the aroma of tender pieces of chicken bathed in a creamy tomato sauce aka Chicken Tikka Masala. This recipe has a traditional creamy tomato-based sauce infused with cumin, ginger, cayenne pepper, cinnamon, and turmeric. The deep earthy, curry spice is added when the chicken breasts are sautéing and blends well during the last simmering phase in the creamy tomato sauce.

Heat the ghee in a large skillet over medium heat. Add the onion and stir until translucent, 5 to 10 minutes. Stir in the garlic and cook until fragrant, about 1 minute. Stir in the cumin, 1 teaspoon salt, cayenne pepper, ginger, cinnamon, and turmeric into the onion mixture and fry until fragrant, about 2 minutes.

Stir the tomato sauce into the onion and spice mixture. Bring to a boil and reduce the heat to low. Simmer the sauce for 10 minutes, then mix in the cream, 1 tablespoon sugar, and paprika. Bring sauce back to a simmer and cook, stirring often, until sauce is thickened, 10 to 15 minutes.

Heat the vegetable oil in a separate skillet over medium heat. Add the chicken into the hot oil. Add the curry powder. Sear the chicken, stirring often, until lightly browned but still pink inside, about 3 minutes.

Transfer the chicken and any pan juices into the sauce. Simmer the chicken in the sauce until no longer pink, about 20 minutes. Adjust the sugar and salt to taste, then garnish with cilantro. Serve with hot rice or naan (if using).

CRAIG CLAIBORNE'S SMOTHERED CHICKEN

- 1 whole chicken, about 3½ pounds
- Fresh cracked black pepper, as needed, to taste
- 2 tablespoons butter
- 2 tablespoons all-purpose flour
- 1½ cups chicken broth

Mississippi's Craig Claiborne is best known for bringing home cooks to the forefront, which he wrote about as the food editor for the New York Times. He referred to his smothered chicken dish as "a food that gives solace to the spirit when you dine on it." Crisping up a peppered spatchcock chicken in a cast-iron skillet and smothering it in a savory pan sauce made with butter, chicken broth, and the leftover drippings is a very restaurant-worthy dish you can easily make at home.

Remove any neck parts and gizzards from the chicken. Then rinse the whole chicken, inside and out, and pat dry with paper towels. To spatchcock the chicken, place the chicken, breast-side down, on a cutting board. The first step to flattening the chicken is to remove the backbone. You can use either a pair of poultry shears or kitchen scissors for this step. Cut along the right of the backbone from the tail to the neck. Next, cut along the left side of the backbone, just as you did on the right side. Keep the backbone piece for future chicken stock or discard. To flatten the bird, break the breastbone. To do this, press down on each of the wings at the same time until the bone cracks. Turn the chicken over so that it lays flat. Your spatchcocked chicken is now ready to be seasoned.

Season the spatchcock chicken with pepper (the chicken broth will provide the salt).

In a very large cast-iron skillet set over low heat, melt the butter. When the butter has melted, place the chicken, breast-side down. Cover the chicken with a plate that fits comfortably inside the skillet. Weight the plate with a heavy can, stone, or brick. The key is to really press the bird while it cooks. Cook until the skin is a deep golden-brown, about 25 minutes. Remove the weight and plate and turn the chicken over. Replace the weight

and plate and cook for 15 minutes. Remove the chicken and set aside. Pour off the fat from the skillet, leaving 2 tablespoons in the pan. Raise the heat to medium and add the flour all at once. Immediately whisk and then while whisking slowly add the chicken broth. Continue to whisk until incorporated and thickened. Reduce the heat back to low, return the chicken, breast-side up, place the weight, and continue to cook until the chicken is exceptionally tender, about another 20 to 30 minutes. Remove from the heat and transfer to a serving platter. Smother with the sauce and serve immediately. Before serving, you can also cut the chicken into serving pieces, then smother with sauce.

Cooking with cast iron is recommended. That's because it's long lasting, and with proper care, will maintain its own natural nonstick coating. Cast iron is also versatile, affordable, and available in all kinds of shapes and sizes.

FRIED CHICKEN WITH CHILE JAM

½ teaspoon white pepper

2 tablespoons chopped fresh cilantro stems

1 tablespoon garlic cloves, peeled (about 3 or 4 cloves)

¼ cup oyster sauce

3 tablespoons fish sauce

2 pounds boneless chicken thighs, skin-on, cut into quarters

1 gallon (16 cups) canola oil, for frying (or less if using a smaller pot)

1¼ cups jasmine rice flour

1 cup soda water

¼ cup Charred Chile Jam, recipe follows

Often the key to exceptional fried chicken is a wet batter, not seasoned flour, so the chicken can marinate properly before being deep-fried. Now toss that crispy golden fried chicken in a home-made charred chile jam crafted from fried shrimp, dried puya chiles, shallots, garlic, sugar, fish sauce, and tamarind water. It's a good Laotian American dish. Quick note on the tamarind water when making the Charred Chile Jam—you can typically find tamarind at Asian markets or online. If you're unable to find it, I've included a recipe below, or you can order the water online. Select the Neya Taste-Imli Pani brand.

Using a stone mortar and pestle, pound the pepper, cilantro, and garlic to a paste. Transfer the paste to a large bowl and add the oyster sauce and fish sauce. Mix well to combine. Add the chicken and toss well to cover the pieces in the marinade. Cover the bowl with plastic wrap and place in the refrigerator for 2 to 12 hours.

In a deep fryer, or deep cooking pot, add the oil over medium-high heat. Note: Use a candy thermometer to get the oil to 350°F. Line a baking sheet with paper towels and have it ready.

In a medium bowl, add the rice flour and soda water. Whisk to combine, creating a smooth batter. Drain the marinated chicken and place in the batter. Coat well and carefully place in the fryer. Cook in batches as to not overcrowd the fryer, which will reduce the temperature of the oil. Fry the chicken until golden-brown and fully cooked, about 5 to 6 minutes per batch. Remove the chicken from the fryer and transfer to the paper-towel-lined baking sheet to drain. When the chicken is finished frying, add the chicken pieces to a large bowl and toss with the Charred Chile Jam. Serve immediately.

Makes 2½ cups

¼ cup dried shrimp

½ cup canola oil plus about ¼ cup, divided

1 cup dried puya chiles (about 4 chiles)

1 cup whole peeled shallots

½ cup peeled garlic cloves

¾ cup granulated sugar

½ cup fish sauce

½ cup tamarind water

CHARRED CHILI JAM

In a sauté pan over medium heat, add the dried shrimp, and toss until fragrant. Remove the shrimp from the pan and set aside. Line a plate with paper towels and set aside. Return the pan over medium heat and add ½ cup of the canola oil. When hot, add the chiles one by one, frying each one until dark red, about 10 to 12 seconds. Remove the chiles and drain them on the paper-towel lined plate. Next, add the shallots one by one, frying each one until brown. Remove the shallots and drain them on the paper-towel lined plate next to the chiles. Repeat the process with the garlic cloves and finally the dried shrimp. Strain the frying oil and add more canola oil to get ½ cup. Using a mortar and pestle, pound the chiles and shrimp until fine. Add the garlic and shallots and continue to pound until a smooth, wet paste is formed. Scrape the paste into a bowl and stir in the sugar, fish sauce, and tamarind water. Add the reserved ½ cup of oil and mix until combined. Use immediately or store in a sealed container in the refrigerator for up to 1 month.

Makes about 2½ cups

3½ ounces tamarind pulp

2½ cups boiling water

TAMARIND WATER

Add the tamarind pulp to a large bowl or container. Slowly pour the boiling water over the tamarind pulp while breaking up with pulp with a fork. Stir well then strain the mixture into another bowl or container using a sieve. Press as much pulp through the sieve as possible using the back of a spoon. Scrape any tamarind puree from the underside of the sieve into the bowl as well.

The tamarind water will keep in the refrigerator for up to 1 week. You can also freeze the water. For easy-to-use portions, pour the water into an ice-cube tray.

Tamarind is a hardwood tree. Native to Africa, it also grows in India, Pakistan, and other tropical regions.

The tree produces bean-like pods filled with seeds surrounded by a fibrous pulp. The pulp begins as green and sour, but as the pod ripens, it becomes juicy and sweeter.

CHICKEN & SAUCE

1½ pounds boneless, skinless chicken thighs, trimmed and cut into ½-inch cubes

¼ cup soy sauce, divided

1 tablespoon cornstarch

1 tablespoon Chinese rice wine or dry sherry

½ teaspoon white pepper

1 tablespoon Chinese black vinegar (find in Asian markets or online)

1 tablespoon packed dark brown sugar

2 teaspoons toasted sesame oil

STIR-FRY

1 tablespoon minced garlic

2 teaspoons grated fresh ginger

2 tablespoons plus 1 teaspoon vegetable oil, divided

½ cup dry-roasted peanuts

5 dried arbol chiles (depending on desired spice level), halved lengthwise and seeded

1 teaspoon Sichuan peppercorns, ground coarse

2 ribs celery, cut into ½-inch pieces

5 scallions, white and light green parts only, cut into ½-inch pieces

KUNG PAO CHICKEN

The secret to a good Kung Pao Chicken—or any great Sichuan dish for that matter—is using the proper seasoning. In this recipe, combine Sichuan pepper and dried arbol chiles. You can shake out the seeds for the right amount of heat you prefer. This version of kung pao is as real as it gets.

Begin by making the chicken and sauce. In a medium bowl, add the chicken, 2 tablespoons of soy sauce, cornstarch, rice wine, and white pepper. Mix well and set aside. In another bowl, add the vinegar, brown sugar, sesame oil, and remaining soy sauce. Mix well and set aside.

For the stir-fry, in another bowl, add the garlic, ginger, and 1 tablespoon of the vegetable oil. Mix well and set aside.

In a large 12-inch nonstick skillet over medium-low heat, add the teaspoon of vegetable oil and dry-roasted peanuts. Cook, stirring constantly, until the peanuts begin to darken, 3 to 5 minutes. Transfer the peanuts to a plate and spread evenly to cool. Return the skillet over medium-low heat and add the remaining tablespoon of vegetable oil. Add the arbol chiles and Sichuan peppercorns. Cook, stirring constantly, until the chiles begin to darken, 1 to 2 minutes. Add the garlic mixture and cook, stirring constantly, until smooth and fragrant, about 30 seconds. Add the chicken in an even layer. Cover the skillet and increase the heat to medium-high. Cook untouched for 1 minute. Remove the cover and add the celery. Cook uncovered, stirring constantly, until the chicken is cooked through, about 2 to 3 minutes. Add the soy sauce mixture and cook, stirring constantly, until the sauce has thickened, and chicken is well coated, about 3 to 5 minutes. Stir in the scallions and peanuts. Transfer to a platter and serve immediately.

L&L DRIVE-INN LIN-KATSU CHICKEN

KATSU CHICKEN SAUCE

2 tablespoons sugar

2 tablespoons distilled vinegar

2 tablespoons vegetable oil

2 tablespoons L&L Barbecue Sauce, recipe follows, or use a store-bought Asian soy-based barbecue sauce

1 tablespoon sesame oil

1½ teaspoons sriracha chili paste

1½ teaspoons Best Foods or Hellmann's Real Mayonnaise

¼ teaspoon minced garlic

¼ teaspoon salt

¼ teaspoon fresh cracked black pepper

8 boneless, skinless chicken thighs

BATTER

1 egg

⅓ cup cornstarch

⅛ teaspoon salt

⅛ teaspoon fresh cracked black pepper

⅛ teaspoon garlic powder

2 to 3 tablespoons water

Vegetable oil, as needed, for frying

2 cups Japanese-style panko breadcrumbs

Classic Katsu Chicken is an Asian favorite. There are many varying recipes, including this one from the former L&L Drive-Inn in Honolulu, Hawaii, which they were famous for. Pieces of boneless chicken are deep-fried for crunch. When making this dish at home, the best temperature to fry the chicken is 340°F. It's also normal for the panko to fall off the chicken, so don't worry too much about that. For the Katsu Sauce, there are a few steps involved, but the result is well worth the time spent in the kitchen. You don't need to make the L&L Barbecue Sauce. You can easily replace it with any Asian soy-based barbecue sauce.

Begin by making the Katsu Chicken Sauce. In a mixing bowl, add the sugar, vinegar, vegetable oil, barbecue sauce, sesame oil, sriracha chili paste, mayonnaise, garlic, salt, and pepper. Mix until well combined. Reserve in the refrigerator until ready to use.

Prepare the chicken thighs. Butterfly them so they spread apart and lie flat. Cut in half if necessary to fit in the frying pan. Set aside.

In a mixing bowl, add the egg, cornstarch, salt, pepper, and garlic powder. Whisk together until combined. Slowly add the water until the batter is smooth and thin.

In a large, deep frying pan, add enough oil to fry the chicken—½ inch of oil is plenty. Heat the oil over medium-high heat, until the oil reaches 340°F.

Dip the pieces of chicken in the batter and then dredge in the panko breadcrumbs. Carefully place each piece in the hot oil. You will likely need to cook the chicken in batches. Fry the chicken until golden-brown on each side, about 5 minutes total for each batch, or until the internal temperature of the chicken reaches 160°F. Use a pair of tongs to turn the chicken pieces to

evenly brown. Remove the chicken from the oil and transfer to a paper-towel-lined platter to drain. Cut each piece of chicken crosswise into strips about ⅝ inch wide and drizzle the Katsu Chicken Sauce over the chicken and serve.

L&L BARBECUE SAUCE

Makes about 1½ cups

½ cup water

½ cup soy sauce

2½ tablespoons sugar

¼ teaspoon garlic powder

⅛ teaspoon fresh cracked black pepper

2 tablespoons all-purpose flour

In small sauce pot, add the water, soy sauce, sugar, garlic powder, and pepper. Whisk until combined. Bring to a simmer over low heat. Then slowly whisk in the flour until the sauce is smooth and thick enough to coat the back of a spoon. The mixture will continue to thicken as it cools. Set aside until ready to use.

OLD-FASHIONED CHICKEN POTPIE

Serves 8

If you haven't realized by now, I like comfort classics, and this old-fashioned favorite is no exception. A mix of rotisserie chicken and vegetables is smothered in a creamy sauce and topped with a sheet of puff pastry. The addition of frozen peas, pearl onions, and corn if you like, streamlines your work in the kitchen by not having to prep a lot of fresh vegetables. This potpie is easy to assemble, making this recipe perfect for beginning cooks and busy families alike.

Preheat the oven to 400°F.

In a large sauté pan or pot over medium-low heat, add the butter. When melted, add the diced onion and sauté until translucent. Add the thyme and continue to sauté for 2 minutes. Add the sherry and let sizzle for a few seconds to burn off the alcohol. Then add the flour and whisk until combined and golden-brown. Whisk in the hot chicken stock, chicken bouillon, and reserved juice from the rotisserie chicken. Add the pepper, nutmeg, hot sauce, parsley, and cream. Stir until thickened. Add the chicken, carrots, pearl onions, and peas. Mix well until heated through. Remove from the heat and transfer the mixture into a 2-quart shallow baking dish.

Next, unfold the thawed pastry sheet on a floured surface. Roll out to a ½-inch overhang of the baking dish. Place the sheet over the dish and crimp the edges. Then brush the pastry with the beaten egg. Make three small slits in the center of the dish for venting while baking.

Place the baking dish into the preheated oven and bake for 20 minutes. Reduce the temperature to 325°F and bake for an additional 20 minutes. Remove from the oven and let cool for at least 12 minutes before serving.

½ cup butter

1 cup finely diced onion

1 teaspoon chopped fresh thyme leaves

1½ tablespoons dry sherry

⅓ cup all-purpose flour

2½ cups hot chicken stock

1 chicken bouillon cube, crushed

1 teaspoon fresh cracked black pepper

¼ teaspoon ground nutmeg

¼ teaspoon hot sauce

¼ cup chopped fresh Italian flat leaf parsley

¼ cup heavy cream

2¼ cups rotisserie chicken, meat picked and chopped (or shredded), juice reserved

1 cup finely chopped carrot, blanched for 2 minutes, or until lightly softened

⅔ cup frozen pearl onions (about 20), thawed and squeezed dry

½ cup frozen petite peas, thawed

1 sheet frozen puff pastry, thawed in refrigerator

1 egg, beaten

PAN-SEARED CHICKEN WITH RIESLING CREAM SAUCE & CHANTERELLES

1 (4-pound) chicken, cut into 8 pieces

Kosher salt, as needed

5 tablespoons butter, divided

1 large red onion, half finely chopped, the other half quartered through the stem

¾ cup white wine (riesling recommended)

1½ cups chicken stock

¾ cup heavy cream

12 ounces chanterelles (or shiitakes), brushed clean, large ones halved lengthwise

Deeply savory, this version on the classic Poulet au Riesling results in pan-seared chicken that's cooked with white wine, cream, and wild mushrooms. This recipe is adapted from chef Antoine Westermann, owner of Paris's and New York City's Le Coq Rico, which focus on fine poultry. For the cooking wine, you can use chardonnay, but it's exceptional with riesling. There are wonderful aromas the wine along with the onion, garlic, and mushrooms emit through the kitchen. You're going to love this one.

Preheat the oven to 350°F.

Season the chicken pieces liberally with salt. In a large Dutch oven over medium heat, add 3 tablespoons of the butter. Once melted and bubbling, add the chicken pieces skin-side down. Work in batches to avoid overcrowding. Cook until the chicken pieces are golden brown, about 10 minutes. Turn and repeat on the remaining side.

Remove the chicken to a baking sheet. Discard all but 1½ tablespoons of the fat from the pot and add the onion. Season with salt and cook, turning the larger onion pieces occasionally and stirring the small pieces, until softened and lightly colored, about 5 minutes. Remove the large pieces to a large-rimmed serving plate. Add the wine to the pot, stirring to deglaze, then cook over medium-high heat until the wine is mostly evaporated, about 2 minutes. Add the stock and heavy cream. Cover and cook at a low simmer for 35 minutes.

During the last 10 minutes of simmering, place the chicken in the oven and roast until a thermometer inserted into the center of the thickest piece reads 155°F, about 10 minutes.

Just before serving, in a large skillet, add the remaining 2 tablespoons of butter over medium-high heat. Once melted and bubbling, add the chanterelles and cook, stirring or shaking the pan occasionally, until browned on the edges and tender throughout, about 8 minutes. Remove to the platter with the reserved red onions.

Taste the sauce and adjust the seasoning as needed. Strain and discard the chopped onions if desired. Pour the sauce onto the serving platter, then nestle the chicken into the sauce. Serve immediately.

PIETRO'S CHICKEN PARMESAN

2 (8-ounce) skinless, boneless chicken breasts

Fresh cracked black pepper, as needed

1¼ cups finely grated fresh Parmigiano-Reggiano cheese, divided

¼ cup all-purpose flour

2 eggs

½ cup vegetable oil

1 cup Marinara Sauce, recipe follows

Looking for a terrific and visually stunning chicken Parm to make at home? Try this restaurant classic, in which you pound the chicken until it's thin and the size of a dinner plate—just like they do at Pietro's on 43rd Street in midtown Manhattan. Then you coat the chicken with Parmesan cheese and breadcrumbs, fry it in a wide skillet until golden brown, and finish under the broiler with homemade marinara and topped with more cheese. It's one of the ultimate comfort foods and brings a lot of smiles because of its enormous size.

Place a chicken breast on a cutting board, breast-side up. Butterfly the chicken by holding a sharp knife parallel to the board. Cut through the breast along the long side, stopping about ½ inch before cutting all the way through. Open the breast like a book, with the connected side acting as the spine. Place the butterflied chicken between two sheets of plastic wrap. Using a kitchen mallet, gently pound the chicken breast until very thin (about ¼ inch) and about 10 inches in diameter, being careful not to tear the meat. Repeat with the other breast, then season both sides of the breasts with pepper.

In a shallow bowl, combine ¾ cup of the cheese and the flour. Lightly beat the eggs in another bowl. Dip each chicken breast in the beaten eggs, then the cheese and flour mixture, shaking off the excess. Place on a baking sheet and repeat with the remaining breast.

Heat the oven to broil.

Heat the oil in a large cast-iron skillet over medium-high heat. When hot, add one breast and cook until the breast is golden-brown, about 1½ minutes. Turn the breast over and cook the other side until golden-brown, another 1½ minutes. Remove the breast from the pan and place on a wire rack placed atop

a foil-lined baking sheet. Repeat the cooking process with the other breast.

Top each chicken breast with ½ cup of the Marinara Sauce, spreading the sauce to the edges, then top with an even layer of the remaining ½ cup Parmigiano-Reggiano cheese. Broil until the cheese is bubbling and the chicken is cooked through, about 2 minutes. Be careful not to over broil the cheese or it will form a hard crust.

MARINARA SAUCE

Heat the oil in a large cast-iron skillet over medium-low heat. When hot, add the onions, and salt, stirring often to avoid browning. Sauté until very soft and translucent, about 8 to 10 minutes. Add the wine and bring to a boil, then cook until the wine is almost completely evaporated, about 4 to 5 minutes. Add the tomatoes and liquid. Reduce heat to low and allow to simmer, stirring occasionally to scrape up the bits at the bottom of the pan, until the tomatoes are tender and the liquid is very concentrated, about 1 hour. Season with pepper. Next, use a kitchen or immersion blender to blend the sauce, being careful not to overwork; you want some chunks. Set aside and keep warm until ready to use.

1 tablespoon olive oil

½ medium white onion, peeled and diced (about ¾ cup)

½ teaspoon salt

¼ cup dry white wine

1 (28-ounce) can San Marzano crushed tomatoes (or use whole peeled tomatoes and crush by hand)

Fresh cracked black pepper

San Marzano tomatoes are a type of plum tomato, often characterized by their elongated shape. They are prized in Italy and across the world for their thick flesh and sweet flavor. San Marzano tomatoes have a lower water content and fewer seeds than other tomatoes, making them a great choice for canning and using in tomato sauces.

ROAST KOJI CHICKEN

2 tablespoons granular
rice koji (available at Asian
markets or online)

1 tablespoon Diamond Crystal
(or 2 teaspoons Morton
kosher salt)

3½–4-pounds chicken,
patted dry

Fresh cracked black pepper,
as needed

This must be one of the most perfectly seasoned roasted chickens I've ever had. That's because of the koji. If you're not familiar, koji is rice grains that have been inoculated with a culture then dried. The science behind it is that koji produces enzymes that convert starches into simple sugars, which breaks down the proteins in the meat, resulting in a bird with strong umami and sweet flavor. Allowing the enzymes to work their magic is the secret to this mouthwatering recipe, which is why it's important to chill your bird in the refrigerator for a considerable amount of time before cooking.

Grind the koji in a spice mill or coffee grinder to a fine powder. Transfer to a small bowl and mix in the salt. Set aside.

Starting at the neck end of the chicken, gently slide your fingers between the skin and breast to loosen skin; continue working down the thighs and legs to fully separate the skin from the meat (be careful not to tear). Rub the koji mixture under the skin all over the meat and inside the cavity, distributing evenly. Season the outside of the chicken liberally with the pepper and place the chicken on a wire rack set inside a rimmed baking sheet. Chill at least 8 hours and for up to 2 days, leaving uncovered up to 24 hours, then loosely covering if chilling longer. Before cooking, allow the chicken to sit at room temperature for 1 hour.

Preheat the oven to 425°F.

Roast the chicken until the skin begins to brown all over, about 20 minutes. If the chicken is browning too quickly, loosely cover with a sheet of aluminum foil. Reduce the oven temperature to 300°F and continue roasting the chicken for 30 to 35 minutes, until an instant-read thermometer inserted into the thickest part of a thigh registers 160°F. Transfer to a cutting board and let rest for at least 15 minutes before carving and serving.

FIVE-STAR

Braised Pork all'Arrabbiata 162

Citrus-Braised Pork with Crispy Shallots 164

Cold-Seared Thick Pork Chops 167

Creole Pork Noodle Soup 168

Goan Pork Vindaloo 170

Haitian Pork Griot 172

Hali'imaile Barbecue Ribs 174

Spicy Grilled Pork with Fennel, Cumin

    & Red Onion 176

Sweet Soy-Lacquered Pork 178

PORK
FROM
EVERYWHERE

BRAISED PORK ALL'ARRABBIATA

2 to 2½ pounds lean boneless pork shoulder, trimmed of fat, cut into 4 pieces

Kosher salt and fresh cracked black pepper, as needed

2 tablespoons extra-virgin olive oil

10 garlic cloves, peeled and smashed

¾ teaspoon red pepper flakes

3 (14-ounce) cans fire-roasted crushed or diced tomatoes

1 cup red wine

5 fresh basil sprigs

2 tablespoons chopped fresh sage (or 2 teaspoons dried)

Here's a sweet and spicy pork dish that features a pork shoulder that's long simmered with fire-roasted tomatoes, red wine, and basil. I like to serve this pork ragù over rigatoni. If you like heat, don't forget a healthy dose of red pepper flakes. It's where the word "Arrabbiata" (meaning "angry" in Italian) comes in.

Heat the oven to 350°F.

Season the pork with 2 teaspoons salt and 1 teaspoon pepper.

In a large Dutch oven over medium-high heat, add the oil. When hot, add the pork shoulder and sear until brown on all sides, about 8 to 10 minutes.

Reduce the heat to medium-low. Add the garlic and red pepper flakes and stir to combine. Add the tomatoes, red wine, basil, and sage. Stir to combine, and season with salt and black pepper. Increase the heat to medium-high and bring to a boil. Once it comes to a boil, remove from the heat, cover, and transfer to the preheated oven. Cook until the pork falls apart, about 2½ to 3 hours. Remove from the oven and working directly in the pot, use two forks to shred the meat into long bite-size pieces. Stir the pork into the tomato sauce until it's evenly distributed. Serve immediately.

CITRUS-BRAISED PORK WITH CRISPY SHALLOTS

3 to 4 pound boneless pork shoulder (Boston butt), cut into 4 large pieces, with fat cap trimmed

Kosher salt, as needed

2 medium oranges

2 tablespoons plus ⅓ cup vegetable oil, divided

6 garlic cloves, peeled and smashed

1 3-inch piece ginger, peeled and finely chopped (about ⅓ cup)

⅓ cup soy sauce

¼ cup mirin

2 tablespoons brown sugar

¼ teaspoon crushed red pepper flakes

3 large shallots, peeled and thinly sliced (about 3 cups)

Steamed jasmine rice, fresh cilantro, and mint leaves, as needed, for serving

Here's an easy pork dish that basically cooks itself. If you have a Dutch oven, this is the perfect recipe for it. That's because you can brown, braise, and simmer large quantities in a Dutch oven, and the vessel retains heat very well, ensuring even cooking while tenderizing the meat. After searing and browning the pork in the Dutch oven, the meat is then slowly simmered with orange peels, orange juice, garlic, ginger, soy sauce, mirin, brown sugar, and red pepper flakes while absorbing the sauce. Heavy browning and cooking until the pork is very soft is the key to this recipe. When the pork becomes fork-tender, it's partially pulled apart, mounded on a bed of rice, and topped with the glossy orange-soy braising liquid. Crispy shallots, cilantro, and mint leaves provide the garnish for this dish.

Pat the pork pieces dry and season all sides with salt. Set aside.

Peel one orange and then cut the peel into large strips. Set the peels aside. Next, slice both oranges in half. Juice the orange halves and strain the juice. You should end up with about ½ cup of juice. Set aside.

In a large heavy pot or Dutch oven over medium-high heat, add the 2 tablespoons of oil. When hot, add the seasoned pork. If necessary, cook in two batches to not overcrowd and cool the pot. Cook the pork, turning occasionally, until very brown on all sides, 8 to 10 minutes per batch. Transfer the pork to a plate if working in batches.

Nestle all the pork pieces back into the pot and add the orange peels, orange juice, garlic, ginger, soy sauce, mirin, brown sugar,

red pepper flakes, and 2 cups water. Bring to a boil. Cover pot, reduce the heat to low, and simmer for 2 hours.

Remove the lid and simmer rapidly until the pork shreds easily when pressed and the sauce is thick enough to coat the pork.

In a medium saucepan over medium-high heat, add the remaining ⅓ cup oil. When hot, add the shallots, cooking, stirring occasionally, until brown and crisp, 6 to 8 minutes. Do not burn the shallots. Transfer the shallots to paper towels to drain and immediately season with salt.

Using a fork, break apart the pork in the pot. To serve, spoon some rice onto serving plates. Divide the shredded pork on top and drizzle the sauce over the top. Garnish with the crispy shallots, along with some fresh cilantro and mint leaves. Serve immediately.

COLD-SEARED THICK PORK CHOPS

Serves 4

Cold searing is an alternate cooking method that does not require an oven, only a cold, dry, nonstick skillet. This unconventional method is a foolproof game changer when it comes to cooking thick cuts of chops (or steaks). They cook in minutes without splattering the stove top. Cold searing cooking also produces moist, tender, well browned chops, with well-cooked pink interiors. The key for this recipe is to be sure the pork chops are at least 1½ inches thick.

Pat the chops dry with paper towels and sprinkle with the pepper. Then arrange the chops in a large 12-inch nonstick skillet, making sure there is plenty of room between and around the chops. Use a larger skillet if necessary.

Place the skillet over high heat and cook the chops for exactly 2 minutes. Turn the chops over and cook for another 2 minutes. Neither side of the chops will be browned at this point, but it's all about the cold-sear process for the perfect chops.

After precisely 2 minutes, turn the chops again, but this time reduce the heat to medium. Continue turning the chops every 2 minutes until the exterior is well browned, the meat is sizzling, and the internal temperature reaches 138°F. Note: The internal temperature will continue to rise to almost 145°F. From start to finish, cooking time should take about 14 to 15 minutes.

Remove the chops and transfer to a carving board and let them rest for 5 minutes. Carve the meat from the bone and slice the meat into ½-inch slices. Season the slices with coarse or flake salt and serve with the bones.

2 (16-ounce) bone-in pork rib chops, 1½ inches thick, trimmed

½ teaspoon fresh cracked black pepper

Coarse or flake salt, as needed

CREOLE PORK NOODLE SOUP

2 tablespoons Worcestershire sauce

2 teaspoons Cajun seasoning

4 garlic cloves, peeled and minced

1½ to 2 pounds lean boneless pork shoulder or butt, trimmed, and cut into 1-inch pieces

4 tablespoons neutral oil, such as canola or vegetable, divided

1 cup chopped celery (from about 2 ribs)

1 medium yellow onion, diced

1 medium green bell pepper, seeded and diced

½ teaspoon kosher salt

2 tablespoons all-purpose flour

1 teaspoon onion powder

1 teaspoon garlic powder

1 teaspoon smoked paprika

½ teaspoon fresh cracked black pepper

¼ teaspoon cayenne powder

¼ teaspoon ground ginger

2 cups beef stock (preferably low-sodium)

8 ounces spaghetti

Resembling a Cajun-style pork stroganoff, this noodle soup is found in many Creole restaurants in New Orleans. Commonly known as "Old Sober" because of its powers to help cure a hangover, this version uses tender chunks of pork instead of beef, and the "soup" is simmered to a sauce, which is then spooned with the pork over spaghetti.

In a medium bowl, add the Worcestershire sauce, Cajun seasoning, and garlic to make a marinade. Mix well to combine, then toss the pork with the marinade. Let sit for at least 30 minutes at room temperature.

As the pork marinates, heat 3 tablespoons of the oil in a large Dutch oven over medium-high heat. Add the celery, onion, bell pepper, and salt. Sauté until translucent, about 5 minutes. Add the flour, onion powder, garlic powder, paprika, pepper, cayenne, and ginger. Sauté for another minute. Transfer the vegetables to small bowl.

Add the remaining 1 tablespoon oil to the pot. Working in batches, sauté the pork over medium-high heat, about 4 minutes on each side, until you get a nice crust on the outside. This is an important step because it chars the meat while sealing in the juices. Add the vegetables and the beef stock to the pot with the pork. Stir well and bring to a boil.

Reduce heat to medium-low and simmer, uncovered, and stirring occasionally, until pork is tender, about 1½ to 2 hours. If the liquid is evaporating too quickly, cover the pot, but try to cook uncovered as much as possible. Taste and adjust for seasoning.

As the pork simmers, set a medium pot of salted water to boil, and, about 10 minutes before serving, add the spaghetti to the pot and cook according to the package directions. Drain the spaghetti.

Serve the noodles, sauce, and pork in bowls.

GOAN PORK VINDALOO

This hot and sour pork vindaloo is a popular Portuguese dish that is often cooked on feast days. It comes together easily, and because the fat forms a sealing layer when refrigerated while the vinegar further intensifies and infuses the pork, it tastes even better after a couple days. A quick tip when chopping the garlic—it's easier to chop if you first crush the cloves. To crush, simply lay the blade of your kitchen knife over the clove and then smack the blade with the heel of your other hand.

- 4 large, dried guajillo chiles, stemmed, seeded, and torn into 1-inch pieces (about 1 ounce total)
- 1 cup water, divided
- 1 (1½ inch) piece fresh ginger, peeled and sliced crosswise ⅛ inch thick (about 1½ tablespoons total)
- 6 garlic cloves, peeled and finely chopped (about 2 tablespoons)
- 1 tablespoon sweet paprika
- 1 tablespoon ground cumin
- 2 teaspoons loose black tea (or 1 or 2 tea bags cut open)
- 2 teaspoons salt
- 1 teaspoon fresh cracked black pepper
- ¼ teaspoon cayenne pepper, optional
- ½ teaspoon ground cinnamon
- ½ teaspoon ground cardamom
- ½ teaspoon ground cloves
- ½ teaspoon ground nutmeg
- 1 (3- to 3½-pound) lean boneless pork butt roast, trimmed, and cut into 1-inch pieces
- 1 tablespoon vegetable oil
- 1 large onion, peeled and finely chopped (about 2 cups)
- ⅓ cup cider vinegar

In a bowl, add the dried chiles and ½ cup water. Place in a microwave and heat for 1½ minutes. Remove and let sit until chiles are soft, about 10 minutes.

Preheat the oven to 325°F.

In a kitchen blender, add the chiles and their water, along with the ginger, garlic, paprika, cumin, tea, salt, pepper, cayenne (if using), cinnamon, cardamom, cloves, and nutmeg. Blend on low speed until a smooth paste forms, about 1½ minutes. With the blender running, add the remaining ½ cup water. Increase the speed to high and mix for 1 minute.

In a large bowl, add the pork and then pour the blended spice mixture over the top. Mix thoroughly.

Add the vegetable oil to a Dutch oven over medium heat. When the oil is hot, add the onion and cook, stirring often, until soft and golden, 7 to 9 minutes. Add the pork mixture and stir to combine with the onion. Continue to cook until the mixture begins to bubble, about another 2 minutes. Cover the pot, transfer to the preheated oven, and cook for 40 minutes. Add the vinegar and stir until combined. Continue to cook until the pork is tender, about another 40 to 50 minutes. Remove from the oven and let stand, uncovered, for 10 minutes. Stir and serve immediately.

½ of 1 small Scotch bonnet or habanero chile (Caution: these are extremely hot)

1 medium onion, peeled and diced (about 1½ cups)

1 small green bell pepper, cored, seeded, and diced (about 1¼ cups)

1 small red bell pepper, cored, seeded, and diced (about 1¼ cups)

¼ cup chopped fresh Italian flat leaf parsley plus more for serving

1 tablespoon kosher salt plus more to taste

1 tablespoon fresh cracked black pepper

6 sprigs fresh thyme plus more thyme leaves for serving

2 garlic cloves, peeled and finely chopped

¼ cup cider vinegar

1 orange, juiced (about ⅓ cup)

1 lemon, juiced (3 tablespoons plus 1 teaspoon)

½ lime, juiced (1 tablespoon)

1 tablespoon Worcestershire sauce

1 (3- to 3½-pound) lean boneless pork shoulder trimmed and cut into 1½-inch pieces

2 tablespoons coconut oil (melted) or olive oil, plus more as needed

Cooked rice, as needed, for serving

HAITIAN PORK GRIOT

Here's a rich and flavorful dish featuring Haiti's most popular meat—pork. Like the other pork recipes in this chapter, this one is easy to prepare. Cubes of pork are soaked in an overnight bath of vinegar and citrus juice that's been seasoned with chiles, onion, bell peppers, parsley, thyme, garlic, and Worcestershire sauce. The pork is then simmered until tender before given a blast under the broiler for caramelization.

Quarter the chile and remove the seeds and membranes. Finely chop one quarter while leaving the rest in whole pieces. Transfer the quartered and chopped chiles to a large Dutch oven with lid. Add the onion, bell peppers, parsley, salt, pepper, thyme, and garlic. Stir in the vinegar, orange juice, lemon juice, lime juice, and Worcestershire sauce. Add the pork and mix well to incorporate. Cover the pot and refrigerate overnight. Remove from the refrigerator at least 1 hour before cooking.

Preheat the oven to 325°F.

Place the Dutch oven over high heat and bring the liquid to a simmer. Cover and transfer to the oven. Cook, stirring occasionally, until the pork is very tender, about 1½ to 2 hours.

Using a slotted spoon, remove the pork and transfer to a rimmed baking sheet. Drizzle the meat with 2 tablespoons of oil, add salt to taste, and toss gently to coat.

Strain the braising liquid, discarding any solids and removing the fat. Return the sauce to the Dutch oven and simmer over high heat until reduced by half, 25 to 30 minutes.

Heat the broiler. Broil the pork, tossing occasionally, until the meat is evenly browned, 5 to 10 minutes. Be careful not to overcook.

To serve, drizzle the pork with additional oil and top with the sauce, fresh parsley, and thyme leaves. Serve on a bed of rice, if desired.

HALI'IMAILE BARBECUE RIBS

This recipe comes from my friend Bev Ganon, whose pork ribs have become famous at her bustling restaurant Hali'imaile General Store in upcountry Maui near Makawao on the way to Haleakalā. This might be the best of all the rib recipes.

Note: No matter how much liquid is used (depending on pan size and amount of ribs), the liquid ratio should remain the same: 1/3 orange juice and 2/3 chicken stock.

Begin my making the sauce. In a heavy saucepan over medium heat, add the margarine. When melted, add the onions and sauté until translucent, 5 to 6 minutes. Add the ketchup, chili sauce, vinegar, brown sugar, mustard, molasses, cayenne pepper, Worcestershire sauce, liquid smoke, and the lemon, lime, and orange juices. Mix well to combine and season with salt and pepper. Bring to a boil, then reduce the heat to low and simmer, uncovered for 2 hours, until thick and reddish brown.

Preheat the oven to 400°F.

Place the rib racks in a roasting pan with the ribs in an upright position. Add orange juice and chicken stock to cover using the appropriate ratio: 1/3 part juice to 2/3 part stock. Then cover the pan with aluminum foil. Bake in the oven for 2 hours.

Prepare an outdoor or gas grill to high heat.

Cut each rib between the bones and slather the ribs in the Hali'imaile Barbecue Sauce. Then place the individual ribs on the grill or under the broiler to finish, turning the ribs to cook all sides. Otherwise, slather the baked ribs heavily with the sauce and place on the grill. Grill for a couple minutes, turn the ribs over, and grill for another couple minutes, until well-marked.

Cut each rib rack into thirds and serve.

HALI'IMAILE BARBECUE SAUCE

2 tablespoons margarine

2 medium onions, peeled and chopped (about 3½ cups)

3 cups ketchup

1½ cups red chili sauce

½ cup cider vinegar

½ cup firmly packed brown sugar

1/3 cup yellow mustard

1/3 cup dark molasses

¾ teaspoon cayenne pepper, or more, depending on desired heat level

1/3 cup Worcestershire sauce

2 teaspoons liquid smoke

½ lemon, juiced (about 1 tablespoon)

½ lime, juiced (about 2 teaspoons)

½ orange, juiced (about 2 tablespoons)

Salt and fresh cracked black pepper, as needed

6 racks of baby back ribs (about 2 pounds each; ribs over 2 pounds won't taste as good)

1/3 part orange juice

2/3 part chicken stock

SPICY GRILLED PORK WITH FENNEL, CUMIN & RED ONION

1¾ pounds lean boneless pork shoulder, trimmed and cut into 1½-inch pieces

Kosher salt, as needed

1 lime, juiced (about 2 tablespoons)

¼ cup fresh cilantro leaves and tender stems, plus more for serving

¼ cup fresh basil leaves and tender stems

2 tablespoons fish sauce

2 garlic cloves, smashed and peeled

1 jalapeño, seeded

1 teaspoon honey

1½ tablespoons fennel seeds

1 tablespoon cumin seeds

1 tablespoon coriander seeds

4 metal or wood (presoaked) skewers

1 medium red onion, quartered and sectioned

Lime wedges, as needed, for garnish

Having an outdoor party? Serve up these grilled pork skewers with fennel, cumin, and red onion. With a good amount of protein, this dish is fun and full of flavor. Should there be any leftovers—there never are at my house—simply store the pork skewers in a tightly sealed container and place them in the refrigerator to enjoy within three or four days.

Season pork lightly with kosher salt and transfer to a bowl or resealable bag.

In a kitchen blender or food processor, add the lime juice, cilantro, basil, fish sauce, garlic, jalapeño, and honey. Blend until the jalapeño and garlic are pureed, then add the fennel, cumin, and coriander. Pulse four or five times to bruise the spices and incorporate into the mixture.

Pour the mixture over the seasoned pork, tossing to coat the pieces. Refrigerate for at least 1 hour and up to 24 hours.

When ready to cook, heat an outdoor or gas grill to high heat.

Thread the pork and red onion onto skewers, alternating as you go and leaving a little space between the pork and onion. Grill over the heat, turning occasionally, until the meat is browned all over and charred in spots and cooked through. The onions should also be well blistered.

Serve the grilled pork and onions with fresh cilantro sprigs on top, and lime wedges on the side for squeezing.

SWEET SOY-LACQUERED PORK

3 tablespoons grapeseed or neutral oil, divided

2 tablespoons finely grated fresh ginger

3 garlic cloves, peeled and finely minced

1 teaspoon fresh cracked black pepper

2 pounds lean boneless pork shoulder or butt, trimmed and cut into 1-inch pieces

¼ cup soy sauce

2 tablespoons light molasses

¼ cup packed brown sugar

¼ cup chicken stock

1 serrano chile, stemmed, seeded, and thinly sliced

4 shallots, peeled and finely chopped (about 1 cup)

1 tablespoon fresh lime juice

½ cup fresh cilantro leaves

Lime wedges, as needed, for garnish

In Bali, braised pork shoulder served with a thick dark soy sauce is a culinary tradition. At my home, braised pork shoulder with some sort of rich lacquered glaze is also popular. Tender pork is coated and slow cooked (braised) in a sauce that's salty and sweet. Use a light molasses for this recipe.

In a medium bowl, add 1 tablespoon of the oil along with the ginger, garlic, and the teaspoon of pepper. Mix well and add the pork. Stir well to coat the pork and set aside.

In a small bowl, add ¾ cup water, soy sauce, molasses, brown sugar, chicken stock, and the sliced chile. Mix well to combine.

In a large skillet over medium-high heat, add the remaining 2 tablespoons of oil. When hot, add the shallots and cook, stirring occasionally, until softened and browned, about 4 to 5 minutes. Add the pork mixture and cook, stirring often, until the meat is no longer pink, about 3 to 4 minutes. Stir in the molasses mixture then bring to a boil. Cover and reduce the heat to medium-low and let simmer until the pork is fork-tender, about 35 to 40 minutes.

Remove the skillet from the heat and skim off any excess fat from the surface. Return the skillet to medium heat and continue to cook, stirring often, until the liquid reduces and becomes saucy, about 10 minutes. Remove from the heat and stir in the lime juice. Transfer to a serving platter and garnish with fresh cilantro and lime wedges. Serve immediately.

FIVE-STAR

Asiago-Crusted Petrale Sole with

Beurre Blanc Sauce 182

Dungeness Crab Bisque 186

Seafood Chowder with Leek, Carrot

& Parsnip.. 190

Steamed Oysters with Garlic, Ginger

& Scallion...194

Veracruz-Style Red Snapper.....................................196

Fish Sauce..198

Tartar Sauce 199

FRESH OFF THE DOCK

ASIAGO-CRUSTED PETRALE SOLE WITH BEURRE BLANC SAUCE

2 pounds petrale sole fillets, or 5-ounce block cut portions when using large fish like halibut

2 teaspoons kosher salt

1 teaspoon freshly cracked black pepper

½ cup 2 percent milk

2 eggs

6 tablespoons fresh Asiago cheese, grated

6 tablespoons fresh Parmigiano-Reggiano cheese, grated

¼ cup Japanese-style panko breadcrumbs, processed fine

¼ cup Clarified Butter, recipe follows (or use store-bought ghee)

¾ cup Beurre Blanc Sauce, recipe follows

2 tablespoons chives, sliced ⅛ inch on the bias, for garnish

1 lemon, cut into 6 slices, for garnish

Cheese-crusted fish with a butter sauce . . . what could be better? With this dish, from Roche Harbor's Chef Bill Shaw, the nutty flavor of the Parmesan combined with the richness of the Asiago seared onto the delicate fish creates an excellent contrast of flavors. When buying petrale sole, ask for larger fillets weighing between 4 and 6 ounces each. If petrale sole is unavailable, my favorite alternative is halibut. Try this recipe with oysters and scallop, as well.

Season the fillets with salt and pepper. In a small bowl, combine the milk and eggs and mix well. Refrigerate.

For the Asiago crust, grate the Asiago and Parmigiano-Reggiano cheeses to a fine powderlike consistency. Using a food processor, add the breadcrumbs and pulse to a fine powderlike consistency as well. Combine the cheese and pureed breadcrumbs in a bowl.

Gently dip the fish fillets in the milk-and-egg mixture, then press into the cheese and panko mixture. Turn the fillets over and repeat. After all the fillets are well crusted, transfer to a plate in a single layer and refrigerate until ready to sauté.

Place a cast-iron pan or griddle over medium-high heat. Add a small amount of Clarified Butter on the hot pan then spread over the entire surface. When the surface of the pan is hot, carefully place the crusted fish in the pan and let cook for 2 to 3 minutes, or until the fish is golden-brown. Turn the fish over, and continue cooking until the fish is firm to the touch and the internal temperature is 120°F.

To serve, arrange the cooked fish on a warm dinner plate and ladle 1 ounce of the Beurre Blanc Sauce over the top of each fillet. Garnish with the chives and lemon slices.

CLARIFIED BUTTER

Makes about 1 cup

4 ounces salted butter

Clarified Butter is easy to make for those of you who have mastered it. The method I use at home starts by unwrapping 2 (4-ounce) butter cubes and placing them in my trusted Pyrex measuring cup. Place the butter in the microwave and heat until the butter is just melted and liquid. Let the warm butter stand for several minutes until you see three distinct layers. The bottom layer is a milky substance, the center layer is a clear yellow color, and the top layer is clear with white salty foam. The center yellow layer is what we are after. To obtain this, the top layer must be poured off and discarded. Don't worry if you discard some of the yellow oil; it's important the top layer is completely removed. The next step is to slowly pour off the yellow oil into a dish without any of the bottom milky layer contaminating it. Once this is done, discard the bottom layer, and your dish containing the yellow oil can now be called Clarified Butter. Keep in a warm place until ready to use.

BEURRE BLANC SAUCE

Makes 1 cup

1 tablespoon peeled and minced shallots

2 tablespoons white wine vinegar

1 cup white wine

½ cup heavy cream

3 sticks butter, cubed and softened at room temperature

¼ teaspoon kosher salt

1 pinch ground white pepper

In a heavy-bottomed saucepan over medium-high heat, add the shallots, vinegar, and wine, and reduce to a light syrup (reducing by approximately 90 percent). Reduce the heat to medium and add the cream. Reduce by half, or ¼ cup. Note: Do not scorch the sauce. Remove from heat if necessary. Reduce the heat to low and whip in the softened butter cubes. We are not melting the butter but softening to form a silky sauce. Season with salt and pepper and keep warm until ready to serve.

Petrale sole is actually a flounder, and considered to be the most flavorful and desirable of Pacific flounders. The fish has a mild, delicately nutty, sweet flavor with small, firm flakes, making petrale sole a great choice for a variety of recipes.

DUNGENESS CRAB BISQUE

1 medium carrot, peeled and chopped (about ½ cup)

1 rib celery, chopped into 1-inch pieces (about ¾ cup)

1 medium red bell pepper, cored, seeded, and chopped (about 1½ cups)

1 medium green bell pepper, cored, seeded, and chopped (about 1½ cups)

1 medium yellow onion, peeled and chopped (about 2 cups)

1 clove garlic, peeled and chopped

1 tablespoon finely chopped fresh Italian flat leaf parsley

½ teaspoon cut (⅛-inch-long) chives

1 teaspoon finely chopped fresh tarragon

1 ounce brandy

3 tablespoons butter

⅓ cup all-purpose flour

2 tablespoons smoked Spanish paprika

¼ cup Old Bay Seasoning

¼ teaspoon fresh cracked black pepper

1 dash cayenne pepper

1 tablespoon crab base

1½ cups whole milk

2¼ cups heavy cream

6 ounces fresh Dungeness crabmeat

1 tablespoon sliced (⅛-inch long) chives, for garnish

This is the very bisque we serve at Roche Harbor Resort. To many, it's one of the best dishes on the menu and one of our most requested recipes which remains unchanged. It's rich, creamy, and loaded with fresh local crab. The Spanish paprika adds a welcoming smoky heat. This bisque can be made two to three days ahead of time by leaving out the milk, heavy cream, and crabmeat, then covering with plastic wrap and storing in the refrigerator. You can purchase the crab base at gourmet food stores or online. Minor's brand is good and, when refrigerated, can last up to about nine months. Better Than Bouillon Fish Base (available at supermarkets and online) is also good.

Place the carrot, celery, red and green bell pepper, onion, and garlic into a food processor. Using the pulse button, pulse the vegetables 5 to 7 times to create a fine mince.

Place a heavy-bottomed, 5-quart saucepan over medium heat and add the minced vegetables along with the parsley, chives, and tarragon. Continue cooking until the vegetables are al dente or firm to the bite. Deglaze the vegetables with the brandy (deglazing the pan detaches the flavorful cooked-on pieces from the bottom of the pan).

Meanwhile, place a saucepan over medium heat and melt the butter. When the butter is melted, add the flour and whisk to form a roux. Continue cooking the roux for 4 to 5 minutes or until the color begins to darken. Allowing the roux to slowly cook over medium heat creates a nutty flavor that enhances soups and sauces. Reserve the roux for the next step.

Continued . . .

Add the paprika, Old Bay Seasoning, black pepper, cayenne, and crab base to the deglazed vegetables and continue cooking over medium heat for 3 to 4 minutes. Add the milk and heavy cream. Continue stirring until the bisque reaches a temperature of 160°F (use a degree probe or digital thermometer to achieve the proper heat).

Add the reserved roux to the bisque and reduce the heat to low. Continue cooking the bisque until a temperature of 180°F is achieved (approximately 30 minutes). Stir frequently to avoid scorching. The bisque should be thick in consistency.

When ready to serve, ladle the bisque into soup bowls and garnish with the fresh Dungeness crab and chives.

Native to the west coast of the United States and Canada, Dungeness crab has long been a favorite of Pacific Northwest chefs. Some compare the crab's succulent meat to that of Maine lobster, but more tender. The sweet, delicate flavor of Dungeness crab is the perfect highlight of your favorite salad, soup, pasta, or seafood dish.

SEAFOOD CHOWDER WITH LEEK, CARROT & PARSNIP

1 cup clam juice

36 medium-size clams (i.e., quahog, cherrystone, littleneck), scrubbed and rinsed

2 tablespoons butter, divided

¼ pound thick-cut bacon, diced

2 tablespoons dulse flakes

2 leeks, tops removed, halved, and cleaned, then sliced into half-moons (about 3 cups)

2 carrots, peeled and halved, then sliced into half-moons (about 1 cup)

2 parsnips, peeled and halved, then sliced into half-moons (about 3 cups)

2 medium-size Yukon Gold potatoes, cubed (about 3½ cups)

1 cup dry white wine

3 sprigs fresh thyme

2 bay leaves

2 cups heavy cream

Fresh ground black pepper, to taste

1 pound firm whitefish fillets (i.e., cod, sea bass), cut into fingers

½ pound sea scallops

¼ cup chopped fresh Italian flat leaf parsley, for garnish

Chowder is to seafood lovers what chili is to meat eaters. They stand by their favorites through thick and thin. This recipe is filled with fresh clams, fish, and sea scallops. The dulse flakes add a savory umami taste to the creamy broth. The chowder also has an intense flavor, and I find it's generally not as lumpy as other seafood chowders.

In a large, heavy Dutch oven over medium-high heat, add about 4 cups water and the clam juice. When hot and bubbling, add the clams and cook until they have opened, 10 to 15 minutes. Any clams that don't open after 15 to 20 minutes should be discarded. Strain the clam broth (about 5 or 6 cups) through a sieve lined with cheesecloth or paper towels and set aside. Remove the clams from their shells and set aside.

Rinse the pot and return to the stove. Add 1 tablespoon of the butter and reduce the heat to medium-low. Add the diced bacon and cook, stirring occasionally, until the fat has rendered, and the bacon has started to brown, about 5 minutes. Use a slotted spoon to remove the bacon and set aside. Add the dulse flakes and leeks to the fat, and cook, stirring frequently, until soft but not brown, about 8 minutes. Add the remaining tablespoon of butter, then stir in the carrots, parsnips, potatoes, and wine, and continue cooking until the wine has evaporated and the vegetables have just started to soften, about 7 minutes. Add enough clam broth (about 5 cups) to cover the potatoes. Add the thyme and bay leaves. Partly cover the pot, and simmer gently until the vegetables are tender (with the potatoes taking the longest), 15 to 20 minutes.

Continued . . .

Meanwhile, chop the clams into bits about the size of the bacon dice. When the vegetables are tender, add the cream and stir in the chopped clams and reserved bacon. Add black pepper to taste. Bring to a simmer (do not boil) and remove and discard the thyme and bay leaves.

If serving immediately, add the fish fingers to the chowder and place the scallops on the surface. Allow the seafood to cook in the heat, 5 to 7 minutes. The chowder is best if it can sit overnight in the refrigerator before adding the fish and scallops. When it's time to serve, reheat the chowder over a low simmer and add the fish and scallops until cooked through. Season to taste with salt and pepper and serve with a garnish of fresh parsley.

STEAMED OYSTERS WITH GARLIC, GINGER & SCALLION

2½ tablespoons vegetable oil, divided

6 tablespoons minced garlic

4 tablespoons peeled and minced fresh ginger

2 tablespoons finely chopped scallion

Sea salt, as needed

Fresh cracked black pepper, as needed

Red pepper flakes, as needed

6 medium to large fresh live oysters in the shell

Scallion slivers, as needed, for garnish

The key to enjoying oysters is to select fresh complementary ingredients. To ensure the oysters you have purchased are fresh, tap the shell. If the shell closes, that means the oyster is still alive. This recipe for steamed oysters (you'll need a steamer basket; I like bamboo) combines the delicate flavors of sautéed ginger, garlic, and scallion.

In a small saucepan over low heat, heat a ½ tablespoon vegetable oil. Add the garlic, ginger, and scallion and season with some salt, pepper, and red pepper flakes, depending on your heat level. Stir frequently to not burn the garlic and ginger. Cook until just browned. Remove from the heat and set aside.

In another small saucepan over medium heat, add the remaining 2 tablespoons of oil and allow it to get hot while preparing the oysters.

Prepare a steamer basket according to manufacturer's instructions (or visit a tutorial online).

Shuck the oysters and place each oyster in the bottom shell. Top each oyster with some of the garlic-ginger mixture. Place the oysters in the steamer basket and steam until firm, about 2 to 3 minutes. Remove the oysters from the steamer and garnish with slivers of scallion. Drizzle half to one teaspoon of the very hot vegetable oil over the top of each oyster. The oysters will sizzle, and the scallion will wilt.

Serve immediately in the shell.

VERACRUZ-STYLE RED SNAPPER

I always enjoy this Mexican-based entrée because it's so good and uncomplicated to prepare. The green olives (I like to use Castelvetrano) complement the capers to enhance the flavors. The addition of jalapeño pepper adds a hint of heat. When making this dish, use either whole red snapper or snapper fillets. If snapper is unavailable, you can replace it with another white flaky fish like halibut or cod. Use about half the sauce while baking the dish and the other half to provide an aromatic seabed to serve the fish (or fillets) in.

Preheat the oven to 425°F.

In a large skillet over medium heat, add the 2 tablespoons of olive oil. When hot, add the onion, stirring, until translucent, about 6 to 7 minutes. Stir in the garlic and cook until fragrant, being careful not to burn, about 30 seconds. Stir in the capers, caper juice, tomatoes, olives, and jalapeño. Cook until the jalapeño softens and the tomatoes begin to blister and collapse, about 3 minutes. Remove from heat and stir in the oregano.

Brush the remaining tablespoon of olive oil in the bottom of a shallow 1-quart baking dish to coat. Spoon about 2 tablespoons of the tomato-olive mixture into the dish, spreading evenly. Top with the fish fillets and season with the pepper and cayenne. Top with the remaining tomato-olive mixture and sprinkle with the lime juice. Place in the preheated oven and bake until the fish is flaky and cooked through, about 12 to 15 minutes. Transfer the fish to serving plates, top with the baked tomato-olive mixture, and serve.

Ingredients

2 tablespoons plus 1 teaspoon olive oil

½ medium white onion, peeled and diced (about 1 cup)

3 cloves garlic, peeled and minced

1 tablespoon capers

1 tablespoon caper juice

1 cup cherry tomatoes, halved

½ cup pitted, sliced green olives (preferably Castelvetrano)

½ jalapeño, seeded and finely chopped

2 teaspoons fresh oregano leaves

2 (6-ounce) fresh red snapper fillets (or other white flaky fish such as halibut or cod), skin removed

⅛ teaspoon fresh cracked black pepper

¼ teaspoon cayenne pepper, or to taste

2 tablespoons fresh lime juice

FISH SAUCE

4 tablespoons butter, divided

2 tablespoons minced shallot

⅔ cup white wine

¼ teaspoon white pepper

1 tablespoon fresh lemon juice

⅓ cup crème fraîche

¼ teaspoon sea salt

Cornstarch, if necessary

Recipes for fish sauce are both innumerable and diverse. Each is generally concocted to enhance the taste of a dish tailored to each cook's palate. Additionally, the ingredients are quite varied. However, many fish sauces contain specific traditional ingredients such as fish, water, wine, lemon, and sea salt. This fish sauce recipe, from the restaurant La Gauloise in Paris, was created to perk the lips but not be over-powerful within the dish.

In a medium sauté pan over medium heat, add one tablespoon of butter. When melted, add the shallots. Sauté, stirring often, until softened, about 2½ minutes. Add the wine and reduce to no more than 25 percent of the original amount, 5 to 6 minutes. Reduce heat to low and add the pepper, lemon juice, crème fraîche, remaining 3 tablespoons of butter, and salt. Move the pan constantly while stirring to avoid scorching. The sauce should be smooth, velvety, and yellow in color. If the sauce appears too thin, add a touch of cornstarch to thicken. Remove from heat and serve immediately with your favorite grilled or sautéed fish.

TARTAR SAUCE

Tartar sauce is customarily served with many seafood dishes. But this accompaniment can raise the flavor bar of other foods such as a wide-ranging assortment of vegetables, baked potatoes, French fries, as a replacement for mayo on a sandwich, as well as a dip for chips and pretzels. What makes tartar sauce super tasty, however, are the components chosen to make it. This recipe includes a variety of ingredients, such as green olives with pimento and capers.

In a food processor, add the pickles, olives, capers, onion, and parsley. Pulse about 8 times, or until finely chopped. Transfer to a mixing bowl, and mix in the mayonnaise, lemon juice, salt, and pepper, until combined. Cover and chill in the refrigerator overnight before serving.

Makes about 2½ cups

½ cup refrigerated dill pickles (about 1 medium to large Claussen), coarsely chopped

4 green olives with pimento

1 tablespoon capers, drained and rinsed

½ cup peeled and chopped yellow onion

¼ cup chopped fresh Italian flat leaf parsley

1¼ cup Best Foods or Hellmann's Real Mayonnaise

1 tablespoon fresh lemon juice

¼ teaspoon kosher salt

¼ teaspoon fresh cracked black pepper

FIVE-STAR

EGGS AND RICE

Baked Denver Omelet...202

   Egg Foo Young 204

   Italian Sausage & Roasted Red Pepper

      Crustless Quiche 206

   Thai Fried Rice...208

   Tortilla de Patatas...210

POTATOES

   Classic Potato Gratin..212

   Thyme-Scented Potato Gratin...........................214

   Extra-Crispy Parmesan-Crusted

      Roasted Potatoes...216

   Mama Moe's Scalloped Potatoes.........................220

   Twice-Baked Potato Casserole............................222

VEGGIES

   Baked Bean Casserole 224

   Melody's Corn Maque Choux 226

   Rich's Sweet Corn Sauté.......................................228

   Roasted Cauliflower Steaks 230

   St. John Beans & Bacon..232

EGGS & RICE, POTATOES & VEGGIES

BAKED DENVER OMELET

2 tablespoons butter

1 large onion, peeled and chopped (about ¾ cup)

½ green bell pepper, cored, seeded, and chopped

1 cup (about 5 ounces) chopped cooked ham, in ¼- to ½-inch cubes

8 eggs

¼ cup milk

½ to 1 cup shredded cheddar cheese (depending on how cheesy you like your omelet)

¼ teaspoon kosher salt

¼ teaspoon fresh cracked black pepper

A baked Denver omelet, also known as a "Western Omelet," is very delicious and quick to make. Similar to a frittata, with onion, bell pepper, ham, and cheddar cheese, this version gets cooked in the oven for about 25 minutes until the eggs are brown and puffy. The result is a light and tasty meal that is filling and satisfying.

Preheat the oven to 400°F.

Grease a 10-inch round baking dish or pie plate.

In a large skillet over medium heat, add the butter. When melted, add the onion and bell pepper, and cook until softened, about 5 minutes. Stir in the ham and cook until heated through, about 5 minutes. Remove from the heat and let cool.

In a bowl, add the eggs and milk and beat well until combined. Stir in the ham mixture, cheese, salt, and pepper. Pour into the prepared dish and bake until the eggs are browned and puffy, about 25 minutes.

Remove from the oven and let cool slightly before serving.

½ cup reduced-sodium chicken broth

1½ tablespoons oyster sauce

1 tablespoon ketchup

1 teaspoon soy sauce

1 teaspoon distilled white vinegar

1 teaspoon cornstarch

¾ teaspoons salt, divided

1 bunch scallions (about ⅓ cup white part, ¾ cup green part)

8 large eggs

1 teaspoon sesame oil

¼ teaspoon fresh cracked black pepper

3 ounces fresh mushrooms, thinly sliced

¾ cup fresh bean sprouts

2 tablespoons vegetable oil

3 ounces peeled and chopped cooked shrimp

EGG FOO YOUNG

Egg Foo Young is a popular Chinese (Cantonese) dish. There are various spellings including Egg Foo Yung and Egg Fu Yung. No matter, Egg Foo Young, also known as a Chinese omelet, is a wonderful, tasty dish. Although it is traditionally made in a wok, it can be pan-fried in a skillet. Egg Foo Young is also flexible. The add-ins can be different types of fish, meats, or vegetables. The most popular meat choices are shrimp, pork, or chicken. This recipe features reduced-sodium chicken broth, oyster sauce, mushrooms, and shrimp. Sesame oil lends a distinctive flavor to the eggs. Toasted sesame oil has a stronger sesame flavor than regular sesame oil—either one works well. After the dish is plated, spread some additional sauce over the top, as the sauce is terrific.

Begin by making the serving sauce. Whisk together the broth, oyster sauce, ketchup, soy sauce, vinegar, cornstarch, and ¼ teaspoon salt in a small heavy saucepan. Bring to a simmer over medium-low heat, whisking occasionally, and simmer for 2 minutes. Remove from the heat.

Chop the scallions, separating the white and green parts. Set aside.

Beat the eggs in a bowl with the sesame oil along with ¼ teaspoon salt, the pepper, and 2 tablespoons of the sauce.

In a 10-inch nonstick skillet over medium-high heat, cook the white part of the scallions, mushrooms, sprouts, and the remaining ¼ teaspoon salt in the vegetable oil until the liquid has evaporated, about 5 minutes. Add the shrimp and half of the scallion greens, then pour in the eggs and cook, stirring occasionally, until the eggs are just cooked but still slightly loose. Cover the skillet and cook until the eggs are just set, about 3 minutes.

Serve sprinkled with the remaining scallion greens. Serve the remaining sauce on the side.

ITALIAN SAUSAGE & ROASTED RED PEPPER CRUSTLESS QUICHE

- 1 tablespoon olive oil
- 7 ounces regular Italian sausage (or hot Italian sausage if you like heat)
- ½ cup diced yellow onion
- ½ teaspoon minced fresh garlic
- 1 cup shredded fontina cheese
- ½ cup shredded fresh Parmigiano-Reggiano cheese
- ½ cup chopped jarred roasted red peppers, patted dry
- 2 tablespoons chopped fresh Italian flat leaf parsley
- 1 teaspoon dried Italian seasoning
- ½ teaspoon fennel seeds, chopped
- ⅛ teaspoon red pepper flakes (or ¼ teaspoon for gentle heat)

CUSTARD

- 8 eggs
- 1 cup whole milk
- 1 cup heavy cream
- ½ teaspoon kosher salt
- ½ teaspoon white pepper
- Pinch ground nutmeg

While there are many versions of this recipe, a true classic is made with old-style seasoned Italian sausage and roasted red peppers. Its ease to prepare makes quiche an excellent choice for a quick weeknight meal, or a weekend get-together. The fontina and Parmesan cheeses, chopped fennel seeds, and red pepper flakes embolden the flavor of the Italian sausage. Oven-warm Italian bread and a side salad with fresh greens make this a recipe nothing short of good old fashioned comfort food. A helpful suggestion when making this meal is to prepare the quiche the evening before and reheat before serving.

Preheat the oven to 325°F.

In a skillet over medium heat, add olive oil. When hot, add the sausage, onion, and garlic and sauté over medium heat until the sausage is cooked through, about 5 minutes. Transfer the sausage mixture to a paper-towel-lined plate, then press dry with additional paper towels, eliminating as much grease as possible.

Add the sausage mixture to a bowl and add the fontina cheese, Parmigiano-Reggiano cheese, roasted red peppers, parsley, Italian seasoning, fennel seeds, and pepper flakes. Mix well to combine and arrange the mixture in a 9- or 10-inch pie plate or round baking dish.

Make the Custard by whisking together in a bowl the eggs, milk, cream, salt, pepper, and nutmeg. Pour the mixture evenly over the sausage-filled plate.

Transfer to the preheated oven and bake until the center is slightly jiggly, about 1 hour, 15 minutes, but check after 1 hour. Cool the dish at least 2 hours before serving.

206

SAUCE

3 tablespoons Thai fish sauce

1 tablespoon oyster sauce

2 tablespoons chicken stock

1 teaspoon garlic chili sauce

1½ teaspoons fresh lime juice

1 teaspoon sugar

FRIED RICE

½ or 1 bacon slice, diced

2 tablespoons vegetable oil

1 medium shallot, peeled and diced (about 3 tablespoons)

3 scallions, chopped, white and green parts separated

3 ounces small cubed cooked ham, chicken and/or shrimp

3 small cloves garlic peeled and minced (about 1 tablespoon),

3 cups day-old (or 2 days old) cooked Jasmine rice

½ cup frozen peas, thawed

2 scrambled eggs, cooked, cooled, and chopped

2 tablespoons dry white wine

THAI FRIED RICE

Thai fried rice is a traditional dish stir-fried in a wok or common frying pan. It is generally mixed with eggs, veggies, meat, or seafood. An authentic Thai fried rice recipe incorporates leftover jasmine rice. Jasmine rice is a long-grain variety that has a nutty flavor. Thai foods customarily do not include soy sauce, but do use an assortment of other savory sauces, most commonly fish sauce, to give them their signature taste. While many have eaten Chinese fried rice, not enough have enjoyed the pleasure of Thai fried rice. Most times it is eaten by itself, but it can be an accompaniment to a main entrée.

Begin by making the Sauce. To a mixing bowl, add the Thai fish sauce, oyster sauce, chicken stock, garlic chili sauce, lime juice, and sugar. Mix well and set aside.

In a large pan over medium-high heat, cook the bacon until three-quarters done, but not crisp. Remove from pan and drain on paper towel. When cool, chop, and set aside.

To the pan with the bacon fat, add the vegetable oil over medium-high heat. Add the shallots and the white parts of the scallions. Sauté until soft, then add the ham and brown slightly. Add the garlic and sauté until fragrant. With a spatula, push the vegetables to the outside of the pan or remove. In the center, add the rice and allow to brown. Add the peas, egg, cooked bacon, green parts of the scallions, and wine. Cook until warmed through. Add the Sauce and stir everything, including the vegetables, until incorporated. Remove from the heat and serve.

TORTILLA DE PATATAS

2½ cups Yukon Gold potatoes

1½ teaspoons kosher salt plus more for seasoning

¼ cup plus 2 tablespoons olive oil, divided

½ medium onion, peeled and chopped (about ¾ cup)

6 to 8 large eggs

Potatoes, onions, and eggs are all you need to prepare this national dish from Spain. The omelet or tortilla de papas is typically served as a small dish or tapas. But I like to prepare this for a light meal. To bring out the depth of the buttery potatoes, cook the onion/ potato mixture until the potatoes have slightly browned. I usually prepare this a couple of hours before mealtime and let it sit at room temperature. This gives me time to make a side dish of fresh greens and fresh chopped avocado and warm up a baguette.

Peel the potatoes, and slice into ¼-inch slices. Place the potatoes in a large bowl, sprinkle with the salt and toss to coat. Transfer the potatoes to a large colander and let stand for 30 minutes or more. Pat dry with paper towels.

Heat ¼ cup of the olive oil in a large nonstick skillet over medium-high heat. Add the potatoes and cook, turning occasionally, until crisp-tender, 10 to 15 minutes.

Add the onions to the potatoes in the skillet and cook until the onions and potatoes are soft, 5 to 8 minutes. Using a slotted spoon, transfer the mixture to a large bowl and let cool slightly. Strain the oil into a heatproof bowl and set aside.

Beat the eggs with 2 tablespoons of the reserved cooking oil from the onions and potatoes until well combined. Add the eggs to the potato mixture and season with salt. Wipe out the skillet and heat the remaining 2 tablespoons olive oil over medium-high heat. Add the egg and potato mixture, arranging the potatoes in the pan to make sure they're submerged.

Reduce the heat to medium and cook the egg-potato mixture until almost set, about 10 minutes. Invert onto a large plate and slide into the skillet browned-side up. Cook until golden on bottom and cooked through, about 4 minutes more. Cut into wedges and serve warm.

CLASSIC POTATO GRATIN

5 garlic cloves, divided

1 tablespoon butter, room temperature

2 medium shallots, peeled and quartered through root ends

2½ cups heavy cream

1 tablespoon kosher salt

1 teaspoon fresh cracked black pepper

1 tablespoon fresh thyme leaves plus more to garnish

4 pounds russet potatoes (about 10 cups), scrubbed, peeled, sliced very thin (⅛ inch) using a mandolin

⅓ cup finely grated fresh Gruyére cheese

2 tablespoons finely grated fresh Parmigiano-Reggiano cheese

With its origins in France, Potato Gratin is one of the most conventional of all the potato-based sides. It can accompany a basic lunch or an exquisite dinner. Thinly slicing the potatoes requires slightly more prep, but it's well worth it. The gratin can be baked a day ahead, covered, and chilled. When ready to prepare, bring to room temperature before broiling. When made as instructed, this creamy smooth, golden-brown dish is packed with an array of taste.

Cut 1 garlic clove in half and rub the inside of a 3-quart shallow baking dish with the cut sides. Smear the butter all over inside of dish. In a small saucepan, bring the shallots, cream, salt, pepper, 1 tablespoon of the thyme leaves, and remaining 4 garlic cloves to a simmer over low heat. Cook until the shallots and garlic are very soft, 15 to 20 minutes. Let cool slightly. Transfer to a blender and blend until smooth.

Preheat oven to 325°F.

Arrange the potato slices in prepared dish, fanning out a handful of slices at a time and placing them in the dish at an angle. This ensures every scoop will have tender potatoes from the bottom and crisp edges from the top. Shingle as you work until the bottom of the dish is covered. Tuck the smaller slices into any gaps to fill. Pour the cream mixture over the potatoes and cover with foil. Transfer to the oven and bake until the potatoes are tender and creamy, 60 to 75 minutes. Remove from the oven and let cool.

Place the oven rack in the highest position in the oven and heat to broil. Remove the foil and top the potatoes with the Gruyère and Parmigiano-Reggiano cheeses. Broil until the cheese is bubbling and the top of the gratin is golden brown, about 5 minutes. Remove from oven and serve topped with more thyme leaves.

212

THYME-SCENTED POTATO GRATIN

This dish is a definite pleaser for any occasion. Be sure to wash the leeks thoroughly as they often contain bits of sand in between the layers. But don't rinse the potato slices since the starch on their surfaces helps to bind and thicken the gratin. Use a mandolin to cut the potatoes into thin, even 1/8-inch slices.

4 tablespoons butter, divided, plus more for greasing baking dish

2 large leeks, white and light green parts only, washed well and thinly sliced (about 3 cups)

3 pounds Yukon Gold potatoes, peeled and sliced into 1/8-inch-thick slices (about 8 cups)

1 cup heavy cream

1 cup whole milk

1 tablespoon kosher salt

1/2 teaspoon white pepper

3 to 4 tablespoons plus 1 teaspoon fresh thyme leaves, divided

1/2 cup grated fresh Gruyère cheese plus 2 tablespoons

1/4 cup grated fresh Parmigiano-Reggiano cheese plus 1 tablespoon

Place 2 tablespoons butter in a large saucepan and heat over medium heat. Add the leeks and sauté until softened but not browned, 4 to 5 minutes.

Add the cream and milk to a saucepan and heat until the mixture simmers. Add the salt and pepper, stirring well to combine. Add the potato slices directly into the hot cream mixture. Press the potato slices gently with a spatula to submerge. Cook, undisturbed, until the potatoes are partially cooked, and the mixture begins to thicken, 10 to 12 minutes. Stir in 3 tablespoons of the thyme leaves.

Preheat the oven to 375°F and place the rack in the center.

Grease a 13 × 9 × 2-inch baking dish with butter. Combine the cheeses in a small mixing bowl. Using a slotted spoon or spider, carefully transfer the potato slices to the prepared baking dish. Carefully pour enough cream mixture to barely cover the potatoes. Dot with remaining 2 tablespoons butter and cover with remaining cheese mixture.

Bake in the preheated oven until the casserole bubbles around the edges and the potatoes are tender and the top is golden brown, 50 to 60 minutes. Note: If the top begins to brown before the potatoes are cooked, cover the gratin with foil.

Remove the gratin from the oven and let sit for 20 minutes. Sprinkle the gratin with the remaining teaspoon of thyme leaves. Slice the gratin into serving portions and transfer to serving plates. Serve immediately.

EXTRA-CRISPY PARMESAN-CRUSTED ROASTED POTATOES

3 pounds russet potatoes, peeled and cut into 1½- to 2-inch chunks

½ teaspoon baking soda

2 tablespoons kosher salt

4 bay leaves

1 tablespoon whole black peppercorns

6 whole garlic cloves, peeled and lightly crushed

3 to 4 fresh thyme or rosemary sprigs, or a mix

3 tablespoons melted butter

1 cup finely grated fresh Parmigiana-Reggiano cheese

Fresh cracked black pepper, as needed

The nutty Parmesan cheese flavor in this recipe makes it a favorite for any Italian or someone who simply savors Parmesan cheese, potatoes, and extra crispy foods. This easy-to-prepare dish can be served as a finger food, or a side dish to prime rib (page 108) or tender steak (page 84).

Preheat the oven to 425°F.

In a large pot over high heat, add the potato chunks, 2 quarts water, baking soda, and salt. Stir to combine.

Cut a 10-by-10-inch square out of cheesecloth and place the bay leaves, peppercorns, garlic, and herb sprigs in the center. Gather up the corners of the cloth into a pouch and tie with butcher's twine. Add the bundle to the pot. Bring the water to a boil, and cook until the potatoes are fork-tender, about 10 minutes after the water comes to a boil.

Drain the potatoes in a colander and discard the aromatic bundle. Line a 13 × 18-inch baking sheet with parchment paper.

Transfer the potatoes to a large bowl. Add the melted butter and cheese. Season lightly with salt and pepper. Toss and fold with a rubber spatula until the butter, cheese, and starch from the potatoes form a slurry over the surface of the potatoes, about 30 seconds. Transfer the potatoes to the prepared baking sheet and spread out so they are mostly separated from one another. Note: At this point, the potatoes can be cooled, then transferred to a sealed container and stored in the refrigerator until ready to roast.

Continued . . .

Transfer the baking sheet to the oven and roast the potatoes until pale golden brown and sizzling on the bottom, about 20 minutes. Flip the potatoes and continue roasting until crisp and golden on most sides, about 15 to 20 minutes longer. Don't allow the potatoes to cook beyond a deep gold, or they will turn bitter.

Remove the potatoes from the oven and allow to cool for 5 minutes before transferring to a serving platter and serving.

Russet potatoes' delicate flavor and fluffy texture makes them ideal for light and fluffy mashed potatoes or fried up crisp and golden brown. Russets are more energy-packed than many vegetables and filled with lots of potassium.

MAMA MOE'S SCALLOPED POTATOES

1 (10.75 ounce) can condensed cream of potato soup

1 (10.75 ounce) can condensed cream of mushroom soup

1 tablespoon Dijon mustard

¼ cup chopped white onion

10 Yukon Gold potatoes (about 3 pounds), thinly sliced, about ⅛ inch on a mandolin

3 cups (about 12 ounces) shredded sharp cheddar cheese

To me, this dish is crazy good. The combination of cheddar cheese and layers of creamy sauce is addicting. The mushroom and potato soups also provide great flavor, which will keep you nibbling even after you're full. If you think roasted garlic mashed potatoes or twice-baked potatoes are delicious, wait until you try Moe's Scalloped Potatoes. As a reminder, it is important to use soft-skinned, buttery-flavored Yukon Gold potatoes with this recipe. You can choose whether or not to peel the potatoes; either way will work for this recipe.

Preheat the oven to 350°F.

Grease a 9 × 13-inch baking dish.

In a microwave-safe bowl, stir together the cream of potato soup, cream of mushroom soup, mustard, and onion. Heat in the microwave until hot, about 3 minutes.

Make a layer with about one-third of the potato slices in the bottom of the prepared dish. Cover with a layer of one third of the soup mixture followed by 1 cup of the cheese. Then repeat the process two more times creating three layers.

Bake covered in the preheated oven for 1 hour. Uncover and continue to bake until the potatoes are fork-tender and the cheese is browned on top, about half an hour. Note: If the top isn't well browned after half an hour, place under the broiler for 1 or 2 minutes, but be careful not to burn the top.

Remove from oven and let cool for 10 minutes before serving.

TWICE-BAKED POTATO CASSEROLE

3 large russet potatoes (a little less than 2½ pounds)

2½ tablespoons plus 1 tablespoon butter, at room temperature

⅓ cup sour cream

2½ tablespoons heavy cream

½ tablespoon salt

½ teaspoon freshly ground black pepper

4 regular slices (about 4 ounces) bacon, cooked, crisp, and crumbled

⅓ cup sharp white cheddar cheese, cut into ½-inch cubes

1 cup (about 4 ounces) mild cheddar cheese, grated, divided

2½ tablespoons finely chopped scallion

1 egg, lightly beaten

Potatoes have a long history. They were first cultivated by the Inca people around 8000 B.C. According to the International Potato Center, potatoes are the third most important food crop for human consumption with more than one billion people eating potatoes worldwide. The versatile baked potato is the staple accompaniment to a wide-ranging number of main course entrées. What makes this casserole so good is its plethora of ingredients—stuffed full of all-time favorites like bacon, cheeses, creams, butter, and more.

Preheat the oven to 400°F.

Scrub the potatoes well and rinse under cool running water. Pat dry with paper towels and prick the potatoes in several places with a fork. Place the potatoes in the oven and bake for 1 hour to 1 hour, 20 minutes, or until tender. Remove from the oven and set aside until cool enough to handle.

When the potatoes have cooled, cut each potato in half horizontally, and, using a spoon or a melon baller, scoop the flesh out of the skins, leaving as little flesh as possible. Place the potato flesh in a large bowl and add the 2½ tablespoons butter, sour cream, heavy cream, salt, and pepper and mash until chunky-smooth. Add the bacon, cubed white cheddar, ½ cup of grated cheddar, scallion, and eggs and mix thoroughly.

Butter an 8 × 8-inch casserole with the remaining tablespoon of butter and reduce the oven temperature to 375°F.

Place the seasoned potato mixture in the prepared casserole dish and top with the remaining ½ cup grated cheddar. Bake for 35 to 40 minutes, or until bubbly around the edges and heated through and the cheese on top is melted and lightly golden. Serve hot.

BAKED BEAN CASSEROLE

6 slices thick cut bacon

1 tablespoon butter

¾ cup chopped yellow onion

¾ cup packed brown sugar

1 teaspoon dry mustard

2 (16- to 18-ounce) cans pork and beans, divided (no less than 4 cups)

½ cup ketchup

Every Fourth of July, I like to make this recipe along with the Picnic Potato Salad (page 37). Everyone will love it, so make plenty, especially if you have a lot of guests to feed; two full recipes will serve about 18 people. For the canned pork and beans, use B&M Original Baked Beans, or your favorite brand.

Preheat the oven to 325°F.

In a large skillet over medium heat, add the bacon and cook until half done. Remove the bacon from the skillet and chop into large pieces and set aside.

In the skillet with the bacon fat, add the butter and chopped onion. Sauté until the onions are soft and translucent. Remove from the heat and set aside.

In a large bowl, add the sugar, dry mustard, pork and beans, and ketchup, along with the bacon and onions. Mix well and pour into a casserole dish.

Cover the dish with aluminum foil and place in the preheated oven. Bake for 1 hour, then remove the foil and bake for an additional hour. Remove from the oven and let cool slightly before serving. Note: The bean mixture will thicken as it cools.

MELODY'S CORN MAQUE CHOUX

7 ears fresh corn

4 slices bacon

3 tablespoons butter

1 cup chopped onion

½ cup diced celery

½ cup diced green bell pepper

½ cup diced red bell pepper

1 tablespoon minced fresh thyme

1 teaspoon kosher salt

½ teaspoon fresh cracked black pepper

¼ teaspoon Creole seasoning

6 cloves garlic, peeled and minced (about 1½ tablespoons)

½ cup beef broth

2 tablespoons chopped fresh Italian flat leaf parsley

During August when corn is ripe, this is a great side dish to serve. Fresh corn on the cob is also available in many markets all year long. This popular side, served in many Southern restaurants, originated, some say, from a blend of old French (Creole) and Native American garden vegetable medleys. This recipe includes Creole seasoning to maintain its authentic flavor of the South. Cooking the corn in the beef broth adds a nice depth to the flavor. To serve as a main dish, simply add some chicken or fish.

Begin by preparing the corn. Stand one ear on its end in a deep dish or bowl to catch the kernels. Carefully slice the kernels off the cob. Then, with the back of the knife, scrape the kernelless cobs to release the corn milk (juice) into the cut kernels. Repeat with the remaining ears. Set aside.

In a large saucepan over medium heat, add the bacon and cook, stirring occasionally, until evenly browned and almost crisp, about 10 minutes. Remove the bacon and drain on paper towels. Reserve 1 tablespoon of the bacon fat from the pan. When the bacon is cool, crumble or chop, and set aside. Next, melt the butter with the bacon fat in the saucepan over medium heat. Add the onion, celery, green bell pepper, red bell pepper, thyme, salt, pepper, and Creole seasoning in the butter mixture until the onions are translucent, about 8 minutes. Stir in the garlic and cook until fragrant, about 2 minutes. Add the beef broth and corn, stir to combine, and bring to a boil. Once boiling, reduce the heat to low and cover the saucepan. Allow to simmer until the broth is nearly evaporated and the vegetables are tender, about 15 minutes. Stir in the reserved bacon fat and fresh parsley and serve.

RICH'S SWEET CORN SAUTÉ

4 ears fresh sweet corn

2 tablespoons butter

¼ cup minced shallot

3 tablespoons heavy cream (or more if you prefer a creamier texture)

Kosher salt and fresh cracked black pepper, as needed

In the late summer, when the corn in my garden is ripe for the picking, I'll make this super simple and quick sauté. Either fresh yellow or white sweet corn can be used. It's not widely known, or accepted, but there isn't much difference in the taste of sweet corn based upon its color—be it yellow, white, or bicolored. Be sure to scrape as much of the corn's milk off the cob as possible. That provides more flavor to the dish.

Begin by preparing the corn. Stand one ear on its end in a deep dish or bowl to catch the kernels. I use the center of a Bundt pan. Carefully slice the kernels off the cob. Then, with the back of the knife, scrape the kernelless cobs to release the corn milk (juice) into the cut kernels. Repeat with the remaining ears. Set aside.

In a large skillet over medium heat, add the butter. When the butter stops foaming, add the shallots and cook until soft and translucent, but do not brown. Add the corn to the pan in an even layer along with any of the milk. Sauté for about 1 minute to warm the corn. Add the heavy cream and stir until the corn is hot and the mixture is thick. Note: Do not overcook or the dish will lose its creaminess. Season with salt and pepper, remove from the heat, and serve.

ROASTED CAULIFLOWER STEAKS

2 heads cauliflower

Extra-virgin olive oil, for drizzling

Garlic salt, as needed

Fresh cracked black pepper, as needed

Grated fresh Parmigiano-Reggiano cheese, as needed

2 tablespoons melted butter

¼ cup minced fresh Italian flat leaf parsley

Cauliflower is wonderful when grilled or roasted. The simple flavors of garlic, pepper, and virgin olive oil enhance the browned caramelized faces of the cauliflower steaks. With the drizzling of butter and topping of freshly minced parsley, vegetarians and nonvegetarians alike will love this recipe.

Preheat the oven to 425°F.

Remove the stems from the cauliflower with a sharp knife, then place the cauliflower heads cut-side down. Slice the cauliflower into ½- to ¾-inch thick steaks (2 heads should yield 3 to 4 steaks). Drizzle each steak with olive oil on both sides and season liberally with garlic salt and pepper. Arrange the seasoned steaks on a greased baking sheet, making sure not to overlap the steaks. Place in the preheated oven and roast for 8 minutes. Using a spatula, carefully turn the steaks over and continue to roast for another 8 minutes, or until the steaks are golden brown and fork-tender. Remove from the oven and transfer the steaks to a serving platter. Top the steaks with a sprinkling of fresh Parmigiano-Reggiano cheese then drizzle the melted butter over the top and garnish with fresh parsley just before serving.

ST. JOHN BEANS & BACON

1 pound (about 7 cups) dried great northern, cannellini, or another white bean, soaked overnight in 8 cups water and drained

1 quart chicken stock

6 garlic cloves, peeled and crushed (2 tablespoons)

2 sprigs each fresh sage, thyme, rosemary, and Italian flat leaf parsley, tied in a bouquet garni

¼ cup duck fat or olive oil

1 pound (about 3½ cups) pancetta, cut into large lardons (about ¼ inch by 1 inch)

2 large white or yellow onions, peeled and chopped (about 5 cups)

2 leeks, trimmed, white and pale green parts, thinly sliced (about 3 cups)

3 ribs celery, thinly sliced (about 1½ cups)

3 tablespoons chopped fresh sage

1 (14-ounce) can Italian plum tomatoes and their juices

Sea salt and fresh cracked black pepper, as needed

St. John Beans and Bacon is a powerhouse dish packed with protein, carbs, vitamins (B_1, B_2, B_3, B_5, B_6, B_{12}, E) and other nutrients. Additionally, the duck fat, which has a rich taste, is more heart-friendly than olive oil. Of course, olive oil will work. The selection of herbs, pancetta, and other ingredients in this hearty flavored recipe offers a fragrant aroma as it simmers.

In a medium pot, add the beans and cover to about 1 inch above the level of the beans with cold water. Bring to a boil over high heat. Once boiling, reduce to a simmer and cook until the beans are soft, but not mushy, about 1½ hours. To the pot, add the chicken stock, garlic, and bouquet garni, and simmer for 30 minutes. Remove from the heat and set aside.

In a large deep pan over low heat, add the duck fat or olive oil. When hot, add the pancetta and cook, stirring occasionally, until evenly browned and crisp, about 20 minutes. Remove the pancetta and drain on paper towels. To the pan, add the onions, leeks, and celery and cook over medium heat until softened, about 10 minutes. Add the chopped sage and tomatoes, crushing the tomatoes in your hands as they're added. Let cook for 15 minutes to thicken the tomatoes, then stir in 1 cup of the simmered stock.

Drain the beans, reserving the stock, and add the beans to the pan. Add the cooked pancetta and 1 additional cup of stock and stir until combined. Taste and season with salt and pepper. Cover the pan and let cook over low heat for 10 to 20 minutes, adding additional stock, one ladleful at a time, if the mixture starts drying out. Remove from oven and let cool slightly before serving.

FIVE-STAR

Magnolia Bakery's Banana Pudding 236

French Silk Pie 238

Monument Cafe's Chocolate Pie 242

Prize-Winning Apple Pie 244

Sugar Cream Pie 246

PUDDING
& FOUR
SWEET PIES

MAGNOLIA BAKERY'S BANANA PUDDING

1 (14-ounce) can sweetened condensed milk

1½ cups ice-cold water

1 (3.4 ounce) package instant vanilla pudding mix

3 cups cold heavy cream

1 (11-ounce) box vanilla wafer cookies (such as Nilla), crumble ⅔ of the cookies, leaving 12 whole

4 to 5 ripe bananas, sliced ⅛-inch thick (use a mandolin)

This incredible dessert, featuring fresh bananas, vanilla wafers, and a fluffy vanilla pudding, has been adapted by Magnolia Bakery in New York. When making this treat and layering the dessert, I like to crumble the wafers rather than leaving them whole.

In the bowl of a stand mixer fitted with the whisk attachment, beat the condensed milk and water on low speed until blended, then increase the speed to medium and whisk until well combined, about 1 minute. Add the instant pudding mix and beat until there are no lumps and the mixture is smooth, about 2 minutes. Transfer the mixture to a medium bowl, cover and refrigerate until firm, at least 1 hour or overnight.

Using the stand mixer with the whisk attachment, whip the heavy cream on medium speed for about 1 minute. Increase the speed to medium-high and whip until stiff peaks form. Be careful not to overwhip.

With the mixer running on low speed, add the pudding mixture a spoonful at a time. Mix until well blended.

In a 4- to 5-quart wide glass bowl or glass baking dish (you can also use 12 (8-ounce) bowls or ramekins), spread one-quarter of the pudding over the bottom and layer up to one-third of the crumbled cookies and one-third of the sliced bananas (enough to cover the layer). If vessel is large enough, repeat the layering two times. End with a final layer of pudding.

Cover tightly with plastic wrap and refrigerate for 4 to 6 hours. Garnish the top with the cookie crumbles or reserved whole cookies, and serve.

CRUST

1½ cups all-purpose flour

¼ cup granulated sugar

½ teaspoon salt

6 tablespoons cold butter, cubed

4 tablespoons cold shortening, cubed

2 tablespoons chilled bourbon

2 to 4 tablespoons ice water

FILLING

4 eggs

⅔ cup granulated sugar

2 tablespoons water

1 cup (8 ounces) semisweet chocolate, finely chopped

1½ sticks (¾ cup) butter, cubed and softened

⅛ teaspoon table salt

WHIP

1 cup heavy cream

2 tablespoons granulated sugar

1 teaspoon pure vanilla extract

FRENCH SILK PIE

People often ask why this pie is called "French Silk?" Essentially, it conveys the pie's velvety and silky texture. For those who appreciate trivia, the original French Silk Pie recipe originated in 1951. Betty Cooper (not Crocker) entered the pie in the third annual Pillsbury Bake-Off competition and won a $1,000 prize for her French Silk Chocolate Pie entry. One thousand dollars was a huge amount of cash back then, so the judges must have really enjoyed her entry. There are many ways to make this dessert—all of which can be labeled delicious. The tender, flaky, bourbon butter-flavored piecrust is terrific.

Begin by making the piecrust. In a mixing bowl, add the flour, sugar, and salt. Cut in the butter and shortening with a pastry blender, until pea sized. Add the bourbon and ice water, 1 tablespoon at a time, while continuing to mix. Add additional ice water if the dough is too dry; dough should seem a bit wet and hold together when squeezed. Transfer the dough to a sheet of parchment paper. Fold the dough over on itself, about 5 times, until the dough comes together. Shape the dough into a disc and wrap in plastic. Chill at least 1 hour, ideally overnight.

Roll out the dough on a floured surface into a 13-inch circle. Transfer the dough to a glass pie plate, pressing into the bottom. Trim the edges to a 1-inch overhang, then roll under and crimp the edges. Prick the bottom of the dough with a fork, and transfer to the refrigerator to chill for 15 minutes.

Preheat the oven to 400°F. Move the oven rack to the lowest level.

To bake, line the crust with a sheet of parchment paper and fill with dried beans or rice to weigh it down. Transfer to the preheated oven and bake until the crust is set, about 15 minutes. Remove from the oven and remove the parchment and beans or rice. Return to the oven and continue to bake until the crust is golden brown, 15 to 18 minutes. Note: If the edges

begin to brown, cover the edges with foil. When finished baking, remove from the oven and let cool before filling.

To make the filling, in a heatproof bowl set over a saucepan over simmering water (do not let bowl touch the water), add the eggs, sugar, and water. Whip the egg mixture with a hand-held mixer until the mixture doubles in size, 10 to 12 minutes. Remove the bowl from the heat and continue beating. Add the chocolate, a little at a time, while whisking until all the chocolate has been added and melted. Allow the mixture to cool, 7 to 10 minutes. Add the cubed butter, several cubes at a time, along with the salt, while continuing to whisk. Set aside.

Make the whipped cream by adding the heavy cream, sugar, and vanilla in a bowl (or use a stand mixer). Whip until the cream until stiff peaks form, about 2 minutes.

Add the whipped cream mixture to the chocolate filling, and fold in until combined. Transfer the filling to the piecrust. Cover and refrigerate for several hours, up to overnight. Let pie stand at room temperature for 30 minutes before serving.

MONUMENT CAFE'S CHOCOLATE PIE

This pie was created in 1995 after the opening of the Monument Cafe in Georgetown, Texas. It soon became the restaurant's renowned signature pie. This version encompasses a wide range of flavors thanks to the combination of semisweet chocolate, grated bittersweet chocolate, a robust dose of heavy cream, and a nutty, snappy delicious crust—all topped with fresh whipped cream and more shaved chocolate.

CRUST

1½ cups pecans, coarsely chopped

¼ cup salted butter

¼ cup packed light brown sugar

FILLING

3 cups heavy cream, divided

¾ cup (6 ounces) semisweet chocolate chips

¾ cup (6 ounces) 60 percent bittersweet chocolate, grated

¼ teaspoon salt

¼ cup granulated sugar

2 teaspoons pure vanilla extract

TOPPING

1 cup cold heavy cream

¼ cup granulated sugar

1 teaspoon pure vanilla extract

Shaved unsweetened chocolate, as needed, for topping

Preheat the oven to 350°F.

Begin by making the crust. On a baking sheet, add the pecans and spread in an even layer, and transfer to the preheated oven. Bake, stirring once, until the pecans are lightly brown, about 10 minutes. Remove from the oven and let cool.

In a medium saucepan, melt the butter. Add the brown sugar and roasted pecans. Mix well until the sugar has dissolved. Remove the chopped pecan mixture and press into a 9-inch pie plate. Transfer to the refrigerator and let set about 1 hour.

To make the filling, in a medium saucepan over high heat, add 1 cup heavy cream and bring to a boil. Remove from the heat and add the chocolate chips, bittersweet chocolate, and salt. Allow to sit for 5 minutes, then stir until smooth. Transfer to a medium bowl and let cool.

In a large bowl, add the remaining 2 cups heavy cream, sugar, and vanilla extract. Beat with a mixer on medium-high speed until stiff peaks form. Fold the mixture into the chocolate, then spread the filling into the crust and refrigerate until set, about 4 hours.

To make the topping, in a large bowl, add the heavy cream, sugar, and vanilla extract. Beat with a mixer on medium-high speed until stiff peaks form. Spread over the pie and top with chocolate shavings.

PRIZE-WINNING APPLE PIE

CRUST

2 cups all-purpose flour

1 teaspoon salt

½ teaspoon baking powder

⅔ cup butter-flavored shortening

1 tablespoon vegetable oil

4 to 5 tablespoons milk

1 egg, beaten, for brushing

FILLING

½ to 1 cup granulated sugar, depending on apple tartness

4 tablespoons cornstarch

½ teaspoon ground nutmeg

1 teaspoon ground cinnamon

¼ teaspoon salt

5 cups thinly sliced peeled tart apples (about 4 or 5 medium-size apples)

2 tablespoons butter

I have baked a wide array of pies in my life, especially apple pies. If you are a fan of tart apples, use Granny Smiths. If you want sweetness in your pie, use Fuji apples. This recipe is quick and easy to prepare and delicious to eat.

Begin by making the crust. In a large mixing bowl, add the flour, salt, and baking powder, and mix well. Cut in the shortening until the mixture resembles small peas. Drizzle in the oil then milk, 1 tablespoon at a time, tossing with a fork after each addition. When the dough is thoroughly mixed, remove the dough from the bowl and press firmly together with your hands. Divide the dough into two balls, then roll out each piece on a lightly floured surface. Place the bottom crust into a 9-inch pie pan and set aside.

To make the filling, in a mixing bowl, add the sugar, cornstarch, nutmeg, cinnamon, salt, and the apples. Mix well until combined, then let stand at room temperature for at least 30 minutes.

Preheat the oven to 400°F.

Add the apple mixture to the dough-lined pan and dot with butter. Cover the pan with the top crust; seal and press the edges of the dough inward, creating a decorative pattern in the top edge of the piecrust. With a knife, slit a couple of steam vents in the top crust and brush the top with the beaten egg. Note: You can cover the edges with aluminum foil to prevent overbrowning.

Transfer the pie to the preheated oven and bake for 25 minutes. Remove the foil and bake for an additional 15 minutes. Remove the pie from the oven and let rest for 15 minutes before serving.

SUGAR CREAM PIE

The ingredients of this pie combine to offer a pastry that is smooth, sweet, rich, and very creamy. The prominent butter and vanilla flavors also impart a pleasing taste and aromatic fragrance.

1 (9-inch) prebaked piecrust (page 238), or use a store-bought piecrust

½ cup granulated sugar plus 1 tablespoon

4 tablespoons cornstarch

2¼ cups heavy cream

6 tablespoons butter, melted

¼ teaspoon ground cinnamon

1 teaspoon pure vanilla extract

In a medium saucepan over medium heat, add the sugar, cornstarch, cream, butter, and cinnamon. Mix well to combine and stir constantly until the mixture becomes thick and creamy, 5 to 7 minutes. Stir in the vanilla and then pour the mixture into the prebaked piecrust. Chill 4 hours, up to overnight. Before serving, preheat the oven broiler on high and move the oven rack to the top position. Sprinkle the pie with 1 tablespoon of sugar. Place under the broiler for 2 to 4 minutes, or until the sugar is brown and bubbly. Let sit for 5 minutes before serving.

ACKNOWLEDGMENTS

James O. Fraioli and Culinary Book Creations, Renee Beachem, Chef William Shaw and Roche Harbor Resort, food photographers Jeff Tucker and Kevin Hossler of Tucker + Hossler Photography, Alan Dino Hebel and Ian Koviak of The Book Designers, editor Varsana Tikovsky, senior editor for Skyhorse Publishing Nicole Frail, and the production team at Skyhorse Publishing. Last but not least, Carolyn Brune, my significant other, who has supported this effort and tasted and suggested along the way.

METRIC CONVERSIONS

If you're accustomed to using metric measurements, use these handy charts to convert the imperial measurements used in this book.

Weight (Dry Ingredients)

1 oz		30 g
4 oz	¼ lb	120 g
8 oz	½ lb	240 g
12 oz	¾ lb	360 g
16 oz	1 lb	480 g
32 oz	2 lb	960 g

Volume (Liquid Ingredients)

½ tsp.		2 ml
1 tsp.		5 ml
1 Tbsp.	½ fl oz	15 ml
2 Tbsp.	1 fl oz	30 ml
¼ cup	2 fl oz	60 ml
⅓ cup	3 fl oz	80 ml
½ cup	4 fl oz	120 ml
⅔ cup	5 fl oz	160 ml
¾ cup	6 fl oz	180 ml
1 cup	8 fl oz	240 ml
1 pt	16 fl oz	480 ml
1 qt	32 fl oz	960 ml

Oven Temperatures

Fahrenheit	Celsius	Gas Mark
225°	110°	¼
250°	120°	½
275°	140°	1
300°	150°	2
325°	160°	3
350°	180°	4
375°	190°	5
400°	200°	6
425°	220°	7
450°	230°	8

Length

¼ in	6 mm
½ in	13 mm
¾ in	19 mm
1 in	25 mm
6 in	15 cm
12 in	30 cm

INDEX

A

almonds
Maytag Blue Cheese Salad, 34–35
apples
Prize-Winning Apple Pie, 244
apricot preserves
Corned Beef Brisket with Apricot Glaze, 92
arbol chiles
Kung Pao Chicken, 144
artichoke hearts
Dungeness Crab & Artichoke Dip, 10
Asiago-Crusted Petrale Sole with Beurre Blanc Sauce, 182–184
avocados
Fredda's Awesome Shrimp de Gallo, 12

B

bacon
Baked Bean Casserole, 224
Braised Chicken with Mustard, 118–120
Corn-Cheddar Chowder, 49
Glazed Meatloaf, 96
Melody's Corn Maque Choux, 226
Pappardelle with Chicken Ragù, Fennel & Peas, 62–64
Seafood Chowder with Leek, Carrot & Parsnip, 190–192
Shannon's Stuffed Mushrooms, 24
Thai Fried Rice, 208
Twice-Baked Potato Casserole, 222
Baked Bean Casserole, 224

Baked Denver Omelet, 202
banana
Magnolia Bakery's Banana Pudding, 236
barbecue sauce
Glazed Meatloaf, 96
L&L Drive-Inn Lin-Katsu Chicken, 146–148
basil
Bev & Joanie's Famous Baked Spaghetti, 54–56
Braised Pork All'arrabbiata, 162
Garden Fresh Tomato Soup, 44
Pasta Puttanesca, 66
Spicy Grilled Pork with Fennel, Cumin 7 Red Onion, 176
bay leaves
Corn-Cheddar Chowder, 49
Mama Leone's Chicken Soup, 46
Mushroom Broth, 42
Old-Fashioned Beef Stew, 98
beans
pork and beans
Baked Bean Casserole, 224
white
St. John Beans & Bacon, 232
bean sprouts
Egg Foo Young, 204
beef
brisket
Brisket in Sweet-and-Sour Sauce, 80–82
Corned Beef Brisket with Apricot Glaze, 92
chuck roast
Classic Pot Roast with Carrot, Celery & Potato, 90–91
Slow Cooker Goulash with Parsley Pasta, 104–106
ground
Beef Stroganoff, 78
Bev & Joanie's Famous Baked Spaghetti, 54–56
Creamy Mushroom Meatloaf, 94

Glazed Meatloaf, 96
Meat Sauce, 68–70
prime rib
Slow-Roasted Prime Rib,
108–110
steak
Prime Beef Poke, 22
stew meat
Old-Fashioned Beef Stew, 98
tenderloin
Chateaubriand with
Chateaubriand Sauce,
84–86
Steak Diane, 112
Beef Stroganoff, 78
beet
Slow Cooker Goulash with
Parsley Pasta, 104–106
bell pepper
Baked Denver Omelet, 202
Bev & Joanie's Famous Baked
Spaghetti, 54–56
Corn-Cheddar Chowder, 49
Creole Pork Noodle Soup, 168
Dungeness Crab Bisque, 186–188
Haitian Pork Griot, 172
Meat Sauce, 68–70
Melody's Corn Maque Choux,
226
Best Tuna Noodle Casserole, 52
Beurre Blanc Sauce, 184
Bev & Joanie's Famous Baked
Spaghetti, 54–56
Bev's Snappy Seafood Salad, 30
blue cheese dressing, 36
Maytag Blue Cheese Salad, 34–35
bourbon
French Silk Pie, 238–240
Braised Chicken Thighs with
Potatoes, Porcini & Cherries,
116–117
Braised Chicken with Mustard,
118–120
Braised Pork All'arrabbiata, 162

brandy
Dungeness Crab Bisque, 186–188
breadcrumbs
Asiago-Crusted Petrale Sole with
Beurre Blanc Sauce, 182–184
Chicken Dijon, 124
Creamy Mushroom Meatloaf, 94
Dungeness Crab Pot Macaroni &
Cheese, 58–60
L&L Drive-Inn Lin-Katsu
Chicken, 146–148
Brisket in Sweet-and-Sour Sauce,
80–82
butter, clarified, 184
buttermilk
Maytag Blue Cheese Dressing, 36

C
cabbage
Pork Lo Mein, 72–74
Cajun seasoning
Creole Pork Noodle Soup, 168
capers
Chicken Piccata with Lemon,
Butter & Caper Sauce, 130–132
Mediterranean Mussels on the
Half Shell, 20
Tartar Sauce, 199
Veracruz-Style Red Snapper, 196
caraway
Slow Cooker Goulash with
Parsley Pasta, 104–106
cardamom
Goan Pork Vindaloo, 170
carrots
Classic Pot Roast with Carrot,
Celery & Potato, 90–91
Corn-Cheddar Chowder, 49
Dungeness Crab Bisque, 186–188
Mama Leone's Chicken Soup, 46
Mushroom Broth, 42
Old-Fashioned Beef Stew, 98
Old-Fashioned Chicken Potpie,
149

Peppercorn-Crusted Roast Beef with Horseradish Cream, 100–102

Seafood Chowder with Leek, Carrot & Parsnip, 190–192

Slow Cooker Goulash with Parsley Pasta, 104–106

Split Pea Soup with Ham, 48

casserole
Baked Bean Casserole, 224
Best Tuna Noodle Casserole, 52
Twice-Baked Potato Casserole, 222

cauliflower
Roasted Cauliflower Steaks, 230

cayenne
Chef John's Salt-Roasted Chicken, 122
Chicken Tikka Masala, 134
Corn-Cheddar Chowder, 49
Creole Pork Noodle Soup, 168
Dungeness Crab Bisque, 186–188
Goan Pork Vindaloo, 170
Hali'imaile Barbecue Ribs, 174
Veracruz-Style Red Snapper, 196

Charred Chili Jam, 142

Chateaubriand with Chateaubriand Sauce, 84–86

cheese
Asiago
Asiago-Crusted Petrale Sole with Beurre Blanc Sauce, 182–184
Stuffed Tiny Potatoes, 26
blue
Maytag Blue Cheese Dressing, 36
Maytag Blue Cheese Salad, 34–35
cheddar
Baked Denver Omelet, 202
Best Tuna Noodle Casserole, 52
Corn-Cheddar Chowder, 49

Dungeness Crab Pot Macaroni & Cheese, 58–60
Mama Moe's Scalloped Potatoes, 220
Twice-Baked Potato Casserole, 222
cream cheese
Corn-Cheddar Chowder, 49
Gruyère
Classic Potato Gratin, 212
Thyme-Scented Potato Gratin, 214
Parmigiano-Reggiano
Asiago-Crusted Petrale Sole with Beurre Blanc Sauce, 182–184
Bev's Snappy Seafood Salad, 30
Chicken Dijon, 124
Chicken Piccata with Lemon, Butter & Caper Sauce, 130–132
Classic Potato Gratin, 212
Dungeness Crab & Artichoke Dip, 10
Dungeness Crab Pot Macaroni & Cheese, 58–60
Extra-Crispy Parmesan-Crusted Roasted Potatoes, 216–218
Garlic Cream Sauce, 70
Glazed Meatloaf, 96
Italian Sausage & Roasted Red Pepper Crustless Quiche, 206
Pappardelle with Chicken Ragù, Fennel & Peas, 62–64
Pasta Puttanesca, 66
Pietro's Chicken Parmesan, 154–156
Roasted Cauliflower Steaks, 230
Shannon's Stuffed Mushrooms, 24

Thyme-Scented Potato Gratin, 214

Chef John's Salt-Roasted Chicken, 122

cherries
Braised Chicken Thighs with Potatoes, Porcini & Cherries, 116–117

chervil
Mediterranean Mussels on the Half Shell, 20

chicken
breasts
Chicken Dijon, 124
Chicken Francese, 126–128
Chicken Piccata with Lemon, Butter & Caper Sauce, 130–132
Pietro's Chicken Parmesan, 154–156
Chef John's Salt-Roasted Chicken, 122
Craig Claiborne's Smothered Chicken, 136–138
Mama Leone's Chicken Soup, 46
Pan-Seared Chicken with Riesling Cream Sauce & Chanterelles, 150–152
Roast Koji Chicken, 158
rotisserie
Old-Fashioned Chicken Potpie, 149
Thai Fried Rice, 208
thighs
Braised Chicken Thighs with Potatoes, Porcini & Cherries, 116–117
Braised Chicken with Mustard, 118–120
Fried Chicken with Chile Jam, 140–142
Kung Pao Chicken, 144
L&L Drive-Inn Lin-Katsu Chicken, 146–148

Pappardelle with Chicken Ragù, Fennel & Peas, 62–64
Chicken Dijon, 124
Chicken Francese, 126–128
Chicken Piccata with Lemon, Butter & Caper Sauce, 130–132
Chicken Tikka Masala, 134
Chile-Braised Short Ribs, 88

chili paste
Prime Beef Poke, 22

chocolate
semisweet
French Silk Pie, 238–240
unsweetened
Monument Cafe's Chocolate Pie, 242

cilantro
Chicken Tikka Masala, 134
Citrus-Braised Pork with Crispy Shallots, 164–166
Fredda's Awesome Shrimp de Gallo, 12
Fried Chicken with Chile Jam, 140–142
Spicy Grilled Pork with Fennel, Cumin 7 Red Onion, 176
Sweet Soy-Lacquered Pork, 178
Watermelon & Charred Tomato Salad, 38

cinnamon
Chicken Tikka Masala, 134
Goan Pork Vindaloo, 170
Prize-Winning Apple Pie, 244
Sugar Cream Pie, 246
Citrus-Braised Pork with Crispy Shallots, 164–166

clams
Classic Clam Linguine, 61
Seafood Chowder with Leek, Carrot & Parsnip, 190–192
Classic Clam Linguine, 61
Classic Potato Gratin, 212
Classic Pot Roast with Carrot, Celery & Potato, 90–91

cloves
    Brisket in Sweet-and-Sour
        Sauce, 80–82
    Goan Pork Vindaloo, 170
cognac
    Chateaubriand with
        Chateaubriand Sauce, 84–86
cola
    Brisket in Sweet-and-Sour
        Sauce, 80–82
    Corned Beef Brisket with Apricot
        Glaze, 92
Cold-Seared Thick Pork Chops, 167
cookies
    vanilla wafer
        Magnolia Bakery's Banana
            Pudding, 236
coriander
    Slow Cooker Goulash with
        Parsley Pasta, 104–106
    Spicy Grilled Pork with Fennel,
        Cumin 7 Red Onion, 176
corn
    Corn-Cheddar Chowder, 49
    Melody's Corn Maque Choux,
        226
    Rich's Sweet Corn Sauté, 228
Corn-Cheddar Chowder, 49
Corned Beef Brisket with Apricot
    Glaze, 92
crabmeat
    Dungeness Crab & Artichoke
        Dip, 10
    Dungeness Crab Bisque, 186–188
    Dungeness Crab Pot Macaroni &
        Cheese, 58–60
crackers
    Glazed Meatloaf, 96
Craig Claiborne's Smothered
    Chicken, 136–138
cream
    Beef Stroganoff, 78
    Best Tuna Noodle Casserole, 52
    Braised Chicken with Mustard,
        118–120

Chicken Tikka Masala, 134
Classic Potato Gratin, 212
Corn-Cheddar Chowder, 49
Cream of Mushroom Soup,
    40–42
Creamy Mushroom Meatloaf, 94
Dungeness Crab Bisque, 186–188
French Silk Pie, 238–240
Garlic Cream Sauce, 60, 70
Italian Sausage & Roasted Red
    Pepper Crustless Quiche, 206
Magnolia Bakery's Banana
    Pudding, 236
Mama Leone's Chicken Soup, 46
Monument Cafe's Chocolate Pie,
    242
Old-Fashioned Chicken Potpie,
    149
Pan-Seared Chicken with
    Riesling Cream Sauce &
    Chanterelles, 150–152
Pappardelle with Chicken Ragù,
    Fennel & Peas, 62–64
Rich's Sweet Corn Sauté, 228
Seafood Chowder with Leek,
    Carrot & Parsnip, 190–192
Steak Diane, 112
Sugar Cream Pie, 246
Thyme-Scented Potato Gratin,
    214
Twice-Baked Potato Casserole,
    222
cream of mushroom soup
    Mama Moe's Scalloped Potatoes,
    220
Cream of Mushroom Soup, 40–42
cream of potato soup
    Mama Moe's Scalloped Potatoes,
    220
Creamy Mushroom Meatloaf, 94
Creamy Mushroom Sauce, 94
crème fraîche
    Braised Chicken Thighs with
        Potatoes, Porcini & Cherries,
        116–117

Braised Chicken with Mustard, 118–120
Fish Sauce, 198
Creole Pork Noodle Soup, 168
Creole seasoning
  Melody's Corn Maque Choux, 226
croutons
  Split Pea Soup with Ham, 48
cucumber
  Prime Beef Poke, 22
cumin
  Chicken Tikka Masala, 134
  Goan Pork Vindaloo, 170
  Slow Cooker Goulash with Parsley Pasta, 104–106
  Spicy Grilled Pork with Fennel, Cumin 7 Red Onion, 176
curry powder
  Chicken Tikka Masala, 134

D
daikon
  Lavender Honey Shrimp, 16–18
dill
  Cream of Mushroom Soup, 40–42
dip
  Dungeness Crab & Artichoke Dip, 10
duck fat
  St. John Beans & Bacon, 232
Dungeness Crab & Artichoke Dip, 10
Dungeness Crab Bisque, 186–188
Dungeness Crab Pot Macaroni & Cheese, 58–60

E
egg
  Baked Denver Omelet, 202
  Best Tuna Noodle Casserole, 52
  Italian Sausage & Roasted Red Pepper Crustless Quiche, 206
  Maytag Blue Cheese Salad, 34–35
  Mediterranean Mussels on the Half Shell, 20
  Thai Fried Rice, 208
  Tortilla de Patatas, 210
  Twice-Baked Potato Casserole, 222
Egg Foo Young, 204
Extra-Crispy Parmesan-Crusted Roasted Potatoes, 216–218

F
fennel bulbs
  Pappardelle with Chicken Ragù, Fennel & Peas, 62–64
fennel seeds
  Italian Sausage & Roasted Red Pepper Crustless Quiche, 206
  Spicy Grilled Pork with Fennel, Cumin 7 Red Onion, 176
fish
  Seafood Chowder with Leek, Carrot & Parsnip, 190–192
  Veracruz-Style Red Snapper, 196
fish sauce, 198
  Fried Chicken with Chile Jam, 140–142
  Spicy Grilled Pork with Fennel, Cumin 7 Red Onion, 176
  Thai Fried Rice, 208
five-spice powder
  Pork Lo Mein, 72–74
Fredda's Awesome Shrimp de Gallo, 12
French Silk Pie, 238–240
Fried Chicken with Chile Jam, 140–142
Fried Pickles with Spicy Mayo, 14

G
Garden Fresh Tomato Soup, 44
garlic
  Bev & Joanie's Famous Baked Spaghetti, 54–56

Braised Chicken Thighs with Potatoes, Porcini & Cherries, 116–117

Braised Pork All'arrabbiata, 162

Brisket in Sweet-and-Sour Sauce, 80–82

Chateaubriand with Chateaubriand Sauce, 84–86

Chicken Dijon, 124

Chicken Tikka Masala, 134

Citrus-Braised Pork with Crispy Shallots, 164–166

Classic Clam Linguine, 61

Classic Pot Roast with Carrot, Celery & Potato, 90–91

Creole Pork Noodle Soup, 168

Dungeness Crab Bisque, 186–188

Dungeness Crab Pot Macaroni & Cheese, 58–60

Extra-Crispy Parmesan-Crusted Roasted Potatoes, 216–218

Fried Chicken with Chile Jam, 140–142

Fried Pickles with Spicy Mayo, 14

Garden Fresh Tomato Soup, 44

Glazed Meatloaf, 96

Goan Pork Vindaloo, 170

Heirloom Tomatoes with Garlicky White Sauce, 32

Italian Sausage & Roasted Red Pepper Crustless Quiche, 206

Kung Pao Chicken, 144

L&L Drive-Inn Lin-Katsu Chicken, 146–148

Mama Leone's Chicken Soup, 46

Meat Sauce, 68–70

Melody's Corn Maque Choux, 226

Mushroom Broth, 42

Pasta Puttanesca, 66

Peppercorn-Crusted Roast Beef with Horseradish Cream, 100–102

Pork Lo Mein, 72–74

Prime Beef Poke, 22

Slow Cooker Goulash with Parsley Pasta, 104–106

Spicy Grilled Pork with Fennel, Cumin 7 Red Onion, 176

Split Pea Soup with Ham, 48

Steamed Oysters with Garlic, Ginger & Scallion, 194

St. John Beans & Bacon, 232

Sweet Soy-Lacquered Pork, 178

Veracruz-Style Red Snapper, 196

Garlic Cream Sauce, 60, 70

ginger
    Brisket in Sweet-and-Sour Sauce, 80–82
    Chicken Tikka Masala, 134
    Citrus-Braised Pork with Crispy Shallots, 164–166
    Creole Pork Noodle Soup, 168
    Goan Pork Vindaloo, 170
    Kung Pao Chicken, 144
    Pork Lo Mein, 72–74
    Steamed Oysters with Garlic, Ginger & Scallion, 194
    Sweet Soy-Lacquered Pork, 178

Glazed Meatloaf, 96

Goan Pork Vindaloo, 170

guajillo chiles
    Goan Pork Vindaloo, 170

H

Haitian Pork Griot, 172

Hali'imaile Barbecue Ribs, 174

ham
    Baked Denver Omelet, 202
    Split Pea Soup with Ham, 48
    Thai Fried Rice, 208

Heirloom Tomatoes with Garlicky White Sauce, 32

hoisin sauce
    Pork Lo Mein, 72–74

Honey Sauce, 18
    Lavender Honey Shrimp, 16–18

horseradish
Peppercorn-Crusted Roast Beef
with Horseradish Cream,
100–102
Horseradish Cream, 102
hot sauce
Glazed Meatloaf, 96
Maytag Blue Cheese Dressing, 36
Old-Fashioned Chicken Potpie,
149

I
Italian dressing
Bev's Snappy Seafood Salad, 30
Italian Sausage & Roasted Red
Pepper Crustless Quiche, 206

J
jalapeño
Fredda's Awesome Shrimp de
Gallo, 12
Spicy Grilled Pork with Fennel,
Cumin 7 Red Onion, 176

K
ketchup
Beef Stroganoff, 78
Brisket in Sweet-and-Sour
Sauce, 80–82
Egg Foo Young, 204
Hali'imaile Barbecue Ribs, 174
koji
Roast Koji Chicken, 158
Kung Pao Chicken, 144

L
Lavender Honey Shrimp, 16
leeks
St. John Beans & Bacon, 232
Thyme-Scented Potato Gratin,
214
Lemon, Butter & Caper Sauce, 132
liquid smoke
Hali'imaile Barbecue Ribs, 174

L&L Barbecue Sauce, 148
L&L Drive-Inn Lin-Katsu Chicken,
146–148

M
macadamia nuts
candied
Lavender Honey Shrimp, 16–18
Magnolia Bakery's Banana Pudding,
236
Mama Leone's Chicken Soup, 46
Mama Moe's Scalloped Potatoes,
220
Marinara Sauce, 156
marjoram
Pasta Puttanesca, 66
mayonnaise
Best Tuna Noodle Casserole, 52
Chicken Dijon, 124
Dungeness Crab & Artichoke
Dip, 10
Fried Pickles with Spicy Mayo, 14
Heirloom Tomatoes with
Garlicky White Sauce, 32
Honey Sauce, 18
L&L Drive-Inn Lin-Katsu
Chicken, 146–148
Maytag Blue Cheese Dressing, 36
Picnic Potato Salad, 37
Shannon's Stuffed Mushrooms,
24
Stuffed Tiny Potatoes, 26
Tartar Sauce, 199
Maytag Blue Cheese Dressing, 36
Maytag Blue Cheese Salad, 34–35
meatloaf
Creamy Mushroom Meatloaf, 94
Glazed Meatloaf, 96
Meat Sauce, 68–70
Mediterranean Mussels on the Half
Shell, 20
Melody's Corn Maque Choux, 226
microgreens
Lavender Honey Shrimp, 16–18

mint
  Citrus-Braised Pork with Crispy
    Shallots, 164–166
mirin
  Citrus-Braised Pork with Crispy
    Shallots, 164–166
molasses
  Hali'imaile Barbecue Ribs, 174
  Sweet Soy-Lacquered Pork, 178
Monument Cafe's Chocolate Pie,
  242
Mushroom Broth, 42
mushrooms
  Best Tuna Noodle Casserole, 52
  chanterelles
    Pan-Seared Chicken with
      Riesling Cream Sauce &
      Chanterelles, 150–152
  Creamy Mushroom Meatloaf, 94
  cremini
    Beef Stroganoff, 78
    Bev & Joanie's Famous Baked
      Spaghetti, 54–56
    Chateaubriand with
      Chateaubriand Sauce,
      84–86
    Cream of Mushroom Soup,
      40–42
  Egg Foo Young, 204
  porcini
    Braised Chicken Thighs
      with Potatoes, Porcini &
      Cherries, 116–117
    Mushroom Broth, 42
  Shannon's Stuffed Mushrooms, 24
  shiitake
    Chateaubriand with
      Chateaubriand Sauce,
      84–86
    Pork Lo Mein, 72–74
mussels
  Mediterranean Mussels on the
    Half Shell, 20
mustard
  Best Tuna Noodle Casserole, 52

Braised Chicken with Mustard,
  118–120
Brisket in Sweet-and-Sour
  Sauce, 80–82
Chateaubriand with
  Chateaubriand Sauce, 84–86
Chicken Dijon, 124
Corned Beef Brisket with Apricot
  Glaze, 92
Glazed Meatloaf, 96
Hali'imaile Barbecue Ribs, 174
Mama Moe's Scalloped Potatoes,
  220
Maytag Blue Cheese Dressing, 36
Mediterranean Mussels on the
  Half Shell, 20
Peppercorn-Crusted Roast Beef
  with Horseradish Cream,
  100–102
Picnic Potato Salad, 37
Steak Diane, 112
mustard powder
  Baked Bean Casserole, 224
  Beef Stroganoff, 78
  Cream of Mushroom Soup,
    40–42

N
naan
  Chicken Tikka Masala, 134
noodles. See also pasta
  Beef Stroganoff, 78
  Best Tuna Noodle Casserole, 52
  Pork Lo Mein, 72–74
nutmeg
  Best Tuna Noodle Casserole, 52
  Goan Pork Vindaloo, 170
  Italian Sausage & Roasted Red
    Pepper Crustless Quiche, 206
  Old-Fashioned Chicken Potpie,
    149
  Prize-Winning Apple Pie, 244

O
Old-Fashioned Beef Stew, 98

Old-Fashioned Chicken Potpie, 149
olives
    Fredda's Awesome Shrimp de
        Gallo, 12
    Pasta Puttanesca, 66
    Veracruz-Style Red Snapper, 196
omelet
    Baked Denver Omelet, 202
oranges
    Citrus-Braised Pork with Crispy
        Shallots, 164–166
    Hali'imaile Barbecue Ribs, 174
oregano
    Heirloom Tomatoes with
        Garlicky White Sauce, 32
    Mama Leone's Chicken Soup, 46
    Meat Sauce, 68–70
    Pasta Puttanesca, 66
    Veracruz-Style Red Snapper, 196
oysters
    Steamed Oysters with Garlic,
        Ginger & Scallion, 194
oyster sauce
    Egg Foo Young, 204
    Fried Chicken with Chile Jam,
        140–142
    Pork Lo Mein, 72–74
    Thai Fried Rice, 208

P
pancetta
    St. John Beans & Bacon, 232
panko
    Asiago-Crusted Petrale Sole with
        Beurre Blanc Sauce, 182–184
    Chicken Dijon, 124
    Dungeness Crab Pot Macaroni &
        Cheese, 58–60
    L&L Drive-Inn Lin-Katsu
        Chicken, 146–148
Pan-Seared Chicken with Riesling
    Cream Sauce & Chanterelles,
    150–152
Pappardelle with Chicken Ragù,
    Fennel & Peas, 62–64

paprika
    Braised Chicken with Mustard,
        118–120
    smoked
        Creole Pork Noodle Soup, 168
        Dungeness Crab Bisque,
            186–188
        Split Pea Soup with Ham, 48
    sweet
        Chicken Tikka Masala, 134
        Goan Pork Vindaloo, 170
        Mama Leone's Chicken Soup,
            46
parsley
    Beef Stroganoff, 78
    Bev & Joanie's Famous Baked
        Spaghetti, 54–56
    Braised Chicken with Mustard,
        118–120
    Chateaubriand with
        Chateaubriand Sauce, 84–86
    Chicken Dijon, 124
    Chicken Francese, 126–128
    Classic Clam Linguine, 61
    Dungeness Crab Bisque, 186–188
    Dungeness Crab Pot Macaroni &
        Cheese, 58–60
    Glazed Meatloaf, 96
    Haitian Pork Griot, 172
    Italian Sausage & Roasted Red
        Pepper Crustless Quiche, 206
    Meat Sauce, 68–70
    Mediterranean Mussels on the
        Half Shell, 20
    Melody's Corn Maque Choux,
        226
    Old-Fashioned Chicken Potpie,
        149
    Pappardelle with Chicken Ragù,
        Fennel & Peas, 62–64
    Pasta Puttanesca, 66
    Prime Beef Poke, 22
    Roasted Cauliflower Steaks, 230
    Seafood Chowder with Leek,
        Carrot & Parsnip, 190–192

Slow Cooker Goulash with Parsley Pasta, 104–106
St. John Beans & Bacon, 232
Tagliatelle Bolognese, 68–70
Tartar Sauce, 199
Parsley Pasta, 106
parsnips
Seafood Chowder with Leek, Carrot & Parsnip, 190–192
pasta. *See also* noodles
angel-hair
Bev's Snappy Seafood Salad, 30
Bev & Joanie's Famous Baked Spaghetti, 54–56
Classic Clam Linguine, 61
Creole Pork Noodle Soup, 168
Dungeness Crab Pot Macaroni & Cheese, 58–60
Pappardelle with Chicken Ragù, Fennel & Peas, 62–64
Slow Cooker Goulash with Parsley Pasta, 104–106
Tagliatelle Bolognese, 68–70
Pasta Puttanesca, 66
pastry
Old-Fashioned Chicken Potpie, 149
peanuts
Kung Pao Chicken, 144
peas
Best Tuna Noodle Casserole, 52
Old-Fashioned Chicken Potpie, 149
Pappardelle with Chicken Ragù, Fennel & Peas, 62–64
split
Split Pea Soup with Ham, 48
Thai Fried Rice, 208
pea sprouts
Lavender Honey Shrimp, 16–18
pecans
Monument Cafe's Chocolate Pie, 242
Peppercorn-Crusted Roast Beef with Horseradish Cream, 100–102

pickles
Fried Pickles with Spicy Mayo, 14
Picnic Potato Salad, 37
pie
French Silk Pie, 238–240
Monument Cafe's Chocolate Pie, 242
Prize-Winning Apple Pie, 244
Sugar Cream Pie, 246
Pietro's Chicken Parmesan, 154–156
pimento
Tartar Sauce, 199
pork
butt
Creole Pork Noodle Soup, 168
Goan Pork Vindaloo, 170
chops
Cold-Seared Thick Pork Chops, 167
ground
Creamy Mushroom Meatloaf, 94
Glazed Meatloaf, 96
shoulder
Braised Pork All'arrabbiata, 162
Citrus-Braised Pork with Crispy Shallots, 164–166
Creole Pork Noodle Soup, 168
Haitian Pork Griot, 172
Spicy Grilled Pork with Fennel, Cumin 7 Red Onion, 176
Sweet Soy-Lacquered Pork, 178
pork and beans
Baked Bean Casserole, 224
Pork Lo Mein, 72–74
potatoes
Braised Chicken Thighs with Potatoes, Porcini & Cherries, 116–117
Classic Potato Gratin, 212
Classic Pot Roast with Carrot, Celery & Potato, 90–91
Extra-Crispy Parmesan-Crusted Roasted Potatoes, 216–218

Mama Moe's Scalloped Potatoes, 220
Old-Fashioned Beef Stew, 98
Picnic Potato Salad, 37
Stuffed Tiny Potatoes, 26
Thyme-Scented Potato Gratin, 214
Tortilla de Patatas, 210
Twice-Baked Potato Casserole, 222
Prime Beef Poke, 22
Prize-Winning Apple Pie, 244
pudding
Magnolia Bakery's Banana Pudding, 236
puya chiles
Fried Chicken with Chile Jam, 140–142

Q
quiche
Italian Sausage & Roasted Red Pepper Crustless Quiche, 206

R
radicchio
Lavender Honey Shrimp, 16–18
ribs
baby back
Hali'imaile Barbecue Ribs, 174
pork ribs
Pork Lo Mein, 72–74
short ribs
Chile-Braised Short Ribs, 88
rice
Citrus-Braised Pork with Crispy Shallots, 164–166
Haitian Pork Griot, 172
Thai Fried Rice, 208
Rich's Sweet Corn Sauté, 228
Roasted Cauliflower Steaks, 230
Roast Koji Chicken, 158
rosemary
Bev & Joanie's Famous Baked Spaghetti, 54–56

Chateaubriand with Chateaubriand Sauce, 84–86
Creamy Mushroom Meatloaf, 94
Peppercorn-Crusted Roast Beef with Horseradish Cream, 100–102
St. John Beans & Bacon, 232

S
sage
Braised Pork All'arrabbiata, 162
St. John Beans & Bacon, 232
salad
Bev's Snappy Seafood Salad, 30
Maytag Blue Cheese Salad, 34–35
Picnic Potato Salad, 37
Watermelon & Charred Tomato Salad, 38
sausage
Italian
Bev & Joanie's Famous Baked Spaghetti, 54–56
Italian Sausage & Roasted Red Pepper Crustless Quiche, 206
Meat Sauce, 68–70
scallops
Seafood Chowder with Leek, Carrot & Parsnip, 190–192
Scotch bonnet chile
Haitian Pork Griot, 172
Seafood Chowder with Leek, Carrot & Parsnip, 190–192
serrano chile
Sweet Soy-Lacquered Pork, 178
Shannon's Stuffed Mushrooms, 24
sherry
Beef Stroganoff, 78
Best Tuna Noodle Casserole, 52
Kung Pao Chicken, 144
Old-Fashioned Chicken Potpie, 149
shrimp
Bev's Snappy Seafood Salad, 30
Fredda's Awesome Shrimp de Gallo, 12

Fried Chicken with Chile Jam,
140–142
Lavender Honey Shrimp, 16–18
Thai Fried Rice, 208
Shrimp Marinade, 18
Lavender Honey Shrimp, 16–18
Slow Cooker Goulash with Parsley
Pasta, 104–106
Slow-Roasted Prime Rib, 108–110
snapper, red
Veracruz-Style Red Snapper, 196
soup
Corn-Cheddar Chowder, 49
Cream of Mushroom Soup,
40–42
Creole Pork Noodle Soup, 168
Dungeness Crab Bisque, 186–188
Garden Fresh Tomato Soup, 44
Mama Leone's Chicken Soup, 46
Seafood Chowder with Leek,
Carrot & Parsnip, 190–192
Split Pea Soup with Ham, 48
sour cream
Beef Stroganoff, 78
Braised Chicken Thighs with
Potatoes, Porcini & Cherries,
116–117
Maytag Blue Cheese Dressing, 36
Peppercorn-Crusted Roast Beef
with Horseradish Cream,
100–102
Slow Cooker Goulash with
Parsley Pasta, 104–106
Twice-Baked Potato Casserole,
222
soy sauce
Brisket in Sweet-and-Sour
Sauce, 80–82
Citrus-Braised Pork with Crispy
Shallots, 164–166
Kung Pao Chicken, 144
L&L Drive-Inn Lin-Katsu
Chicken, 146–148
Pork Lo Mein, 72–74

Sweet Soy-Lacquered Pork, 178
Spicy Grilled Pork with Fennel,
Cumin 7 Red Onion, 176
spinach
Mama Leone's Chicken Soup, 46
Split Pea Soup with Ham, 48
sriracha
Fried Pickles with Spicy Mayo, 14
Glazed Meatloaf, 96
L&L Drive-Inn Lin-Katsu
Chicken, 146–148
Steak Diane, 112
Steamed Oysters with Garlic,
Ginger & Scallion, 194
stew
Old-Fashioned Beef Stew, 98
St. John Beans & Bacon, 232
Stuffed Tiny Potatoes, 26
Sugar Cream Pie, 246
Sweet Soy-Lacquered Pork, 178

T
Tagliatelle Bolognese, 68–70
tamarind
Fried Chicken with Chile Jam,
140–142
Tamarind Water, 142
tarragon
Dungeness Crab Bisque, 186–188
Mama Leone's Chicken Soup, 46
Tartar Sauce, 199
tea
black
Goan Pork Vindaloo, 170
Tempura Batter, 18
Lavender Honey Shrimp, 16–18
Thai Fried Rice, 208
thyme
Braised Chicken with Mustard,
118–120
Chateaubriand with
Chateaubriand Sauce, 84–86
Chef John's Salt-Roasted
Chicken, 122

Classic Potato Gratin, 212

Classic Pot Roast with Carrot, Celery & Potato, 90–91

Corn-Cheddar Chowder, 49

Cream of Mushroom Soup, 40–42

Extra-Crispy Parmesan-Crusted Roasted Potatoes, 216–218

Haitian Pork Griot, 172

Mama Leone's Chicken Soup, 46

Melody's Corn Maque Choux, 226

Old-Fashioned Chicken Potpie, 149

Pappardelle with Chicken Ragù, Fennel & Peas, 62–64

Split Pea Soup with Ham, 48

St. John Beans & Bacon, 232

Thyme-Scented Potato Gratin, 214

tomatoes

  Bev & Joanie's Famous Baked Spaghetti, 54–56

  Braised Pork All'arrabbiata, 162

  Fredda's Awesome Shrimp de Gallo, 12

  Garden Fresh Tomato Soup, 44

  Heirloom Tomatoes with Garlicky White Sauce, 32

  Mama Leone's Chicken Soup, 46

  Meat Sauce, 68–70

  Pietro's Chicken Parmesan, 154–156

  Prime Beef Poke, 22

  St. John Beans & Bacon, 232

  Veracruz-Style Red Snapper, 196

  Watermelon & Charred Tomato Salad, 38

tomato sauce

  Bev & Joanie's Famous Baked Spaghetti, 54–56

  Chicken Tikka Masala, 134

  Pasta Puttanesca, 66

  Pietro's Chicken Parmesan, 154–156

Tortilla de Patatas, 210

tuna

  Best Tuna Noodle Casserole, 52

turmeric

  Chicken Tikka Masala, 134

Twice-Baked Potato Casserole, 222

V

veal

  ground

    Creamy Mushroom Meatloaf, 94

    Glazed Meatloaf, 96

Veracruz-Style Red Snapper, 196

vinegar

  apple cider

    Glazed Meatloaf, 96

  Chinese black

    Kung Pao Chicken, 144

  cider

    Brisket in Sweet-and-Sour Sauce, 80–82

    Goan Pork Vindaloo, 170

    Haitian Pork Griot, 172

    Hali'imaile Barbecue Ribs, 174

  red wine

    Maytag Blue Cheese Dressing, 36

    Old-Fashioned Beef Stew, 98

    Slow Cooker Goulash with Parsley Pasta, 104–106

  white

    Egg Foo Young, 204

  white wine

    Asiago-Crusted Petrale Sole with Beurre Blanc Sauce, 184

    Mediterranean Mussels on the Half Shell, 20

W

Watermelon & Charred Tomato Salad, 38

wine

  Chinese rice

Kung Pao Chicken, 144
Pork Lo Mein, 72–74
red
  Braised Pork All'arrabbiata, 162
  Brisket in Sweet-and-Sour
    Sauce, 80–82
  Chateaubriand with
    Chateaubriand Sauce,
    84–86
  Classic Pot Roast with Carrot,
    Celery & Potato, 90–91
  Slow Cooker Goulash with
    Parsley Pasta, 104–106
riesling
  Pan-Seared Chicken with
    Riesling Cream Sauce &
    Chanterelles, 150–152
white
  Braised Chicken with Mustard,
    118–120
  Chef John's Salt-Roasted
    Chicken, 122
  Chicken Francese, 126–128
  Chicken Piccata with Lemon,
    Butter & Caper Sauce,
    130–132

Classic Clam Linguine, 61
Fish Sauce, 198
Mediterranean Mussels on the
  Half Shell, 20
Pappardelle with Chicken
  Ragù, Fennel & Peas, 62–64
Pietro's Chicken Parmesan,
  154–156
Seafood Chowder with Leek,
  Carrot & Parsnip, 190–192
Thai Fried Rice, 208
Worcestershire sauce
  Best Tuna Noodle Casserole, 52
  Classic Pot Roast with Carrot,
    Celery & Potato, 90–91
  Cream of Mushroom Soup,
    40–42
  Creole Pork Noodle Soup, 168
  Glazed Meatloaf, 96
  Haitian Pork Griot, 172
  Hali'imaile Barbecue Ribs, 174
  Maytag Blue Cheese Dressing, 36
  Steak Diane, 112